Philippines:
From Crisis
to Opportunity

COUNTRY ASSISTANCE REVIEW

Gianni Zanini

1999
The World Bank
Washington, D.C.

Copyright © 1999
The International Bank for Reconstruction
and Development/THE WORLD BANK
1818 H Street, N.W.
Washington, D.C. 20433, U.S.A.

Design: The Magazine Group/Jeff Kibler
Photo credits: Shepard Sherbell: cover
          World Bank Photo Library: p. 2, p. 5, p. 28
          Edwin Huffman: p. 18, p. 25

ISBN 0-8213-4294-0

Library of Congress Cataloging-in-Publication Data
Zanini, Gianni, 1954–
Philippines, from crisis to opportunity / [prepared by Gianni Zanini].
p. cm. — (Operations evaluation studies)
At head of title: World Bank Operations Evaluation Department. Country assistance review.
ISBN 0-8213-4294-0
1. Philippines—Economic policy. 2. Philippines—Economic conditions—1986 3. World Bank—
Philippines. 4. Economic assistance—Philippines. I. World Bank. Operations Evaluation Dept.
II. Title. III. Series: World Bank operations evaluation study.
HC453.Z36 1999
338.9599—dc21

99-12535
CIP

 Printed on recycled paper.

Acknowledgments

This Country Assistance Review benefited from comments provided by Bangko Sentral ng Pilipina (BSP). Their kind cooperation and valuable assistance are gratefully acknowledged.

This report was prepared by Gianni Zanini (Task Manager). Major contributors and members of the mission included Per Bastoe (poverty, health, and education, on secondment from the Norwegian government), Yuen Loh Yee (agriculture and natural resource management, on secondment from the Asian Development Bank), Sonomi Tanaka (aid coordination, NGO participation, and gender issues), and Julius Gwyer (portfolio management, statistical annex, and general research assistance). Desk contributions were provided by Raj Chhikkara (financial sector), Gary Wells (quality at entry), Art Bruestle (water supply and sanitation), Jan De Weille (transport), David Greene (energy, health, and education projects), Ron Parker (environment), Edgard Rodriguez (decentralization and SMEs), and Zia Choudhri (PBDDR).

Ponciano Intal (PIDS, Manila); Deena Khatkhate (Bank consultant); Donald Mathieson (IMF); Luis Landau, Nicolas Mathieu, and Luis Ramirez (OEDCR) offered valuable comments on an early draft. Jacqueline Jackson provided administrative assistance.

This report was produced as part of OEDPK's publication series by a team under the direction of Elizabeth Campbell-Pagé, consisting of Leo Demesmaker, Caroline McEuen, Kathy Strauss, and Tsige Kagombe. The design was by The Magazine Group.

Director-General, Operations Evaluation Department:	*Robert Picciotto*
Director, Operations Evaluation Department:	*Elizabeth McAllister*
Acting Manager, Country Evaluations and Regional Relations:	*René Vandendries*
Task Manager:	*Gianni Zanini*

ENGLISH

FOREWORD

Country Assistance Reviews (CARs) are evaluations that take the country as the unit of account and concentrate on the *relevance, efficacy,* and *efficiency* of the Bank's over-all program of assistance, as well as its *sustainability* and its impact on *institutional development.*[1] This CAR examines World Bank assistance to the Philippines since 1986, a turning point in the economic and social policy landscape of that country. The CAR is selective as to time span, instruments, sectors, and issues covered. The focus is on issues that remain relevant today for government and Bank decisionmakers.

The CAR is composed of this *Overview* volume, which summarizes the evidence and presents the key messages and recommendations, and a *Main Report*, which provides supporting analyses, and is available from OED upon request.

The overview synthesizes OED and Bank reports, including Performance Audit and Implementation Completion Reports, Country Assistance Program/Strategy Papers, Country Briefs, Country Economic Memoranda, sector reports, Country Risk Assessments, management briefs for the Annual Meetings and high-level field visits, and project and general country files. The overview is also based on interviews with current and past Filipino officials, including those at the secretary level; academics and private sector representatives; foreign donor representatives; and Bank, International Finance Corporation (IFC), and International Monetary Fund (IMF) staff, conducted between April and Decem-

ESPAÑOL

PREFACIO

Los exámenes de la asistencia a los países son evaluaciones que toman como unidad el país y se concentran en la pertinencia, la eficacia y la eficiencia del programa de asistencia general del Banco, así como en su sostenibilidad y sus efectos en el desarrollo institucional.[1] En el presente examen de la asistencia a un país se analiza la asistencia que el Banco Mundial ha prestado a Filipinas desde 1986, año en que se produjeron cambios decisivos en el panorama de la política económica y social de ese país. El examen es selectivo por lo que se refiere al período, los instrumentos, los sectores y las cuestiones que abarca y se centra en aspectos que siguen siendo pertinentes hoy para los responsables de la adopción de decisiones del Gobierno y del Banco.

El examen de la asistencia al país está compuesto por el presente Panorama general, en el que se resumen los hechos y se presentan las ideas y las recomendaciones fundamentales, y un informe principal en el que figuran análisis de base y que está a disposición de los interesados en el Departamento de Evaluación de Operaciones.

En el Panorama general se resumen los informes del Departamento de Evaluación de Operaciones y del Banco, incluidos los informes de evaluación ex post y de ejecución de los proyectos, los documentos de estrategia y de programas de asistencia, las sinopsis sobre el país, los memorandos económicos, los informes sectoriales, las evaluaciones de riesgos, las sinopsis sobre la gestión para las reuniones anuales y para las visitas de alto nivel al país y la documentación general sobre el proyecto y sobre el país. El Panorama general también se basa en

FRANCAIS

PRÉFACE

Les Études sur l'assistance-pays sont des évaluations dont l'unité de compte est le pays. Ces études servent essentiellement à mesurer la validité, l'efficacité et l'efficience de l'ensemble du programme d'assistance de la Banque, ainsi que sa viabilité et son impact sur le renforcement institutionnel.[1] La présente Étude examine l'aide fournie par la Banque mondiale aux Philippines depuis 1986, année qui a marqué un tournant dans l'évolution de la politique économique et sociale du pays. Elle porte sur une période, des instruments, des secteurs et des sujets bien précis, l'accent étant mis sur les problèmes qui continuent de se poser au gouvernement et aux décideurs de la Banque.

L'Étude se compose de la présente Vue d'ensemble, qui récapitule les faits et expose les principales conclusions et recommandations, ainsi que d'un Rapport principal contenant des analyses explicatives, qui peut être obtenu sur demande auprès du Département de l'évaluation des opérations (OED).

Cette vue d'ensemble décrit brièvement les rapports de l'OED et de la Banque, y compris les Rapports d'évaluation rétrospective et les Rapports de fin d'exécution, les Programmes d'assistance au pays et les Documents de stratégie, les Fiches-pays, les Mémorandums économiques, les rapports sectoriels, les Évaluations du risque-pays, les Notes de gestion préparées en vue des Assemblées annuelles et des missions de haut niveau dans le pays, ainsi que les dossiers sur les projets et sur le pays en général. Elle se fonde également sur les entretiens qui ont eu lieu entre avril et décembre 1997 avec les responsables du gouvernement actuel et des gouvernements précédents,

ENGLISH

ber 1997. The Bank Resident Mission provided excellent facilities and staff assistance for logistics and substantive issues during the CAR mission in June 1997, including two roundtable discussions with Filipino officials involved in decentralization issues and NGO representatives.

1. The first CARs published in the series are for Ghana (1995), Zambia (1996), Argentina (1996), Morocco (1997), Poland (1997), Côte d'Ivoire (1997), and Mozambique (1997).

ESPANOL

las entrevistas que entre abril y diciembre de 1997 se mantuvieron con funcionarios filipinos en activo y con sus predecesores, incluidos funcionarios con nivel de secretario; representantes de medios académicos y del sector privado; representantes de los donantes extranjeros, y personal del Banco, de la Corporación Financiera Internacional (CFI) y del Fondo Monetario Internacional (FMI). La Misión Residente del Banco facilitó unas instalaciones y una asistencia de personal excelentes para cuestiones logísticas y sustantivas durante la misión del examen de la asistencia al país de junio de 1997, incluidos dos debates de mesa redonda con funcionarios filipinos dedicados a cuestiones de descentralización y con representantes de organizaciones no gubernamentales.

1. Los primeros exámenes de la asistencia a los países publicados en esta serie son los correspondientes a Ghana (1995), Zambia (1996), Argentina (1996), Marruecos (1997), Polonia (1997), Côte d'Ivoire (1997), y Mozambique (1997).

FRANCAIS

dont certains ministres, des représentants des milieux universitaires et du secteur privé, des représentants des bailleurs de fonds étrangers, ainsi que des membres du personnel de la Banque, de la Société financière internationale (SFI) et du Fonds monétaire international (FMI). La Mission résidente de la Banque aux Philippines a mis des installations d'excellente qualité à la disposition de l'équipe de l'Étude lors de sa mission de juin 1997 et lui a fourni un appui logistique et une aide sur les questions de fonds, notamment en organisant deux tables rondes avec des responsables philippins s'occupant des questions de décentralisation et de représentation des ONG.

1. Les premières Études publiées dans cette série portaient sur les pays suivants: Ghana (1995), Zambie (1996), Argentine (1996), Maroc (1997), Pologne (1997), Côte-d'ivoire (1997), et Mozambique (1997).

Robert Picciotto
Director-General, Operations Evaluation Department

EXECUTIVE SUMMARY

This Country Assistance Review (CAR) is the eighth of the new country-focused studies that evaluate the relevance, efficacy, and efficiency of the Bank's overall program of assistance, as well as its sustainability and impact on institutional development. The objectives are to establish accountability, derive lessons of experience, and provide recommendations for action. After discussion with the government, a revised report will be distributed without restriction. This CAR concentrates on Bank assistance since 1986, which marks the turning point in the country's economic and social policy frameworks.

Since 1986 the Aquino and Ramos administrations have secured many of the conditions that have characterized the development path trod by the East Asian miracle economies—macroeconomic stability and flexibility, absence of major price distortions, an educated work force, and export orientation. The Philippines can today boast of more openness to foreign investment, less government involvement in the corporate sector, and a stronger banking system.

Despite the political turmoil, natural calamities, and external shocks that beset the country until the early 1990s, the incidence and intensity of poverty have been substantially reduced since 1985. The share of the population living below the international poverty line dropped by 7 percentage points, to below 26 percent. The key indicators of health and education point to substantial progress. In education and gender equity, the Philippines is ahead of most neighboring countries. Gross national

RESUMEN

El presente examen de la asistencia a un país es el octavo de los nuevos estudios centrados en países cuyo objeto es evaluar la pertinencia, eficacia y eficiencia del programa general de asistencia del Banco, así como su sostenibilidad y sus efectos en el desarrollo institucional. Los objetivos del examen son determinar responsabilidades, aprender de la experiencia adquirida y hacer recomendaciones para la acción. Un informe revisado se distribuirá sin restricciones después de las deliberaciones con el Gobierno. El presente examen se concentra en la asistencia prestada por el Banco a partir de 1986, año en que se produjeron cambios decisivos en el marco de la política económica y social del país.

Desde ese año, los gobiernos de Aquino y Ramos han establecido muchas de las condiciones características del camino hacia el desarrollo que han seguido las economías del milagro de Asia oriental—flexibilidad y estabilidad macroeconómica, ausencia de grandes distorsiones de los precios, una población activa instruida y una economía orientada hacia la exportación. Actualmente puede afirmarse que en Filipinas hay más apertura a la inversión extranjera, menos intervención estatal en el sector empresarial y un sistema bancario más sólido.

A pesar de los trastornos políticos, las catástrofes naturales y las conmociones debidas a causas externas que afectaron al país hasta comienzos del decenio de 1990, la incidencia y la intensidad de la pobreza han disminuido sustancialmente desde 1985. El porcentaje de población que vive por debajo del umbral

RÉSUMÉ ANALYTIQUE

La présente analyse est la huitième d'une nouvelle série d'études destinées à évaluer la validité, l'efficacité et l'efficience de l'ensemble de l'aide fournie par la Banque à un pays donné, ainsi que la viabilité de ce programme d'aide et son impact sur le renforcement institutionnel. Ces études ont pour but de renforcer la prise de responsabilités, de tirer les leçons de ce qui a déjà été fait et de formuler des recommandations. Une fois qu'il aura été examiné par le gouvernement, ce rapport sera révisé et fera l'objet d'une large diffusion. La présente Étude analyse l'aide fournie par la Banque aux Philippines depuis 1986, année qui a marqué un tournant dans l'évolution de la politique économique et sociale du pays.

C'est à partir de cette date que les gouvernements Aquino et Ramos ont mis en place un grand nombre des conditions qui ont caractérisé le développement miracle des économies est-asiatiques—souplesse et stabilité macroéconomique, distorsions limitées des prix, main-d'œuvre instruite, orientation vers l'exportation. Les Philippines peuvent aujourd'hui se targuer d'être plus ouvertes aux investissements étrangers, d'avoir réduit le rôle de l'État dans le secteur des entreprises et d'avoir renforcé leur système bancaire.

En dépit des troubles politiques, des catastrophes naturelles et des chocs extérieurs qu'a connus le pays depuis le début des années 90, la prévalence et l'intensité de la pauvreté ont sensiblement diminué depuis 1985. Le pourcentage de la population vivant en-dessous du seuil international de pauvreté a baissé de 7 points et est maintenant inférieur à 26%. Les indicateurs clés en matière de santé et d'éducation témoignent des

ENGLISH

product (GNP) per capita more than doubled, to US$1,190 in 1996. Although modest compared with the East Asian tigers, gross domestic product (GDP) growth since the early 1990s reached above 5 percent in 1996 and again in 1997, despite the fallout from the Asian financial crisis. Price and exchange rate stability have been accompanied by rising money demand, reflecting financial deepening. The engine for economic growth has been private investment, which increased by 6 percentage points to above 20 percent of GDP. According to business surveys, today's institutional environment in the Philippines compares favorably with that of other middle-income countries.

These positive features notwithstanding, judged by some critical factors for economic and social development, the Philippines still fares below the norm for the East Asia region: the country has lower national savings and investment, higher import duties, more rapid population growth, inadequate infrastructure, an inefficient bureaucracy and judicial system, widespread corruption, and general insecurity. Some social development indicators such as incidence of communicable diseases and access by the poor to educational services have regressed in recent years.

On the whole, however, the country's strengths outweigh its fragile elements. Despite the financial turmoil that has engulfed the region, the economy is showing more resilience and maintaining momentum more effectively than its neighbors. The government is committed to completing and deep-

ESPAÑOL

internacional de pobreza se ha reducido siete puntos porcentuales y es ahora inferior al 26%. Los indicadores fundamentales de salud y educación señalan progresos considerables. En cuestiones de educación y de igualdad entre los géneros, Filipinas es un país más avanzado que la mayoría de sus vecinos. El producto nacional bruto (PNB) ha registrado un crecimiento superior al doble de su valor anterior y en 1996 alcanzó los US$1.190. Si bien modesto en comparación con el de los tigres del Asia oriental, el crecimiento del producto interno bruto (PIB) desde principios del decenio de 1990 fue superior al 5% en 1996 y también en 1997, a pesar de los efectos negativos de la crisis financiera de Asia. A la estabilidad de los precios y de los tipos de cambio se ha unido una demanda monetaria creciente, lo que indica que se ha producido una intensificación financiera. El motor del crecimiento económico ha sido la inversión privada, que ha aumentado seis puntos porcentuales hasta alcanzar un valor superior al 20% del PIB. Según las encuestas de coyuntura, el entorno institucional actual de Filipinas es mejor que el de otros países de ingreso mediano.

Pese a esos aspectos positivos, si el país se evalúa sobre la base de otros factores fundamentales para el desarrollo económico y social, sus resultados siguen siendo inferiores a la norma en la región de Asia oriental: el volumen de ahorro y de inversión nacional es menor, los aranceles son más altos, el crecimiento de la población es mayor, la infraestructura es inadecuada, el funcionariado y el sistema judicial son ineficientes, la corrupción está muy extendida y la inseguridad es un mal generalizado. En los últimos años se han producido

FRANÇAIS

progrès substantiels qui ont été accomplis. En ce qui concerne l'équité dans le domaine de la parité hommes-femmes ou de l'éducation, les Philippines sont en avance sur la plupart de leurs voisins. Le produit national brut (PNB) par habitant a plus que doublé pour atteindre 1 190 dollars en 1996. Bien que modeste au regard de celle des tigres est-asiatiques, la croissance du produit intérieur brut (PIB) a dépassé les 5%, une première fois en 1996, puis de nouveau en 1997, et ce, malgré les retombées de la crise financière en Asie. La stabilité des prix et des taux de change s'est accompagnée d'une demande croissante de monnaie, laquelle témoigne de la diversification des circuits financiers. Le moteur de la croissance économique reste l'investissement privé, qui a gagné 6 points pour représenter plus de 20% du PIB. D'après des enquêtes réalisées auprès de chefs d'entreprise, l'environnement institutionnel philippin soutient aujourd'hui favorablement la comparaison avec celui d'autres pays à revenu intermédiaire.

Malgré ces progrès, les Philippines se situent encore en-deçà de la norme en Asie de l'Est, si on en juge par certains facteurs d'une importance critique pour le développement socio-économique: ainsi, les taux d'épargne et d'investissement intérieurs sont plus faibles que dans l'ensemble de la région, et les droits sur les importations, plus élevés; la croissance démographique est plus forte; les équipements d'infrastructure sont inadéquats; la fonction publique et le système judiciaire sont inefficaces; la corruption est répandue; et il règne un climat général d'insécurité. Certains indicateurs du développement social, comme l'incidence des maladies

ENGLISH

ening the reform agenda.

During the past dozen years, the Bank assistance strategy has moved from economic recovery to poverty alleviation, in line with government and Bank priorities. But this shift started only in the mid-1990s with new operations in support of elementary education and agrarian reform. Bank assistance has been both relevant and satisfactory at the macro level, and in private sector (including small and medium-size enterprises, SMEs) development, financial sector strengthening, and municipal development. But its relevance and efficacy in other sectors has been uneven. Assistance results have ranged from relevant and marginally satisfactory in some sectors (water and sanitation, and transport) to barely relevant or unsatisfactory in others (health, education, agriculture, energy, and decentralization).

Bank projects have performed relatively well. Ratings for completed projects are almost at par with the East Asia and Pacific Region (EAP) for outcome and sustainability, and even better for institutional development impact. At completion, all adjustment loans (US$1.4 billion) since the mid-1980s have received a satisfactory outcome and likely sustainability ratings. All but one received a substantial institutional development rating. For investment lending (US$4.2 billion), the picture is also positive. But Bank performance in identification, appraisal, and supervision remains below the EAP average.

The current portfolio of 23 projects ($2.2 billion) appears to be performing even better, with satisfactory ratings above 90 percent, in

ESPANOL

regresiones en algunos indicadores del desarrollo social, como la incidencia de las enfermedades transmisibles y el acceso de las personas pobres a los servicios de educación.

No obstante, en conjunto, los aspectos positivos superan las deficiencias del país. A pesar de los trastornos financieros que ha sufrido la región, la economía de Filipinas está dando muestras de mayor resistencia y está manteniendo su impulso más eficazmente que las de los países vecinos. El Gobierno ha adoptado el compromiso de finalizar y profundizar el programa de reformas.

En los últimos 12 años, la estrategia de asistencia del Banco ha pasado de centrarse en la recuperación económica a hacerlo en el alivio de la pobreza, en consonancia con las prioridades del Gobierno y del Banco. Pero este cambio no empezó a producirse hasta mediados del decenio de 1990, con nuevas operaciones de apoyo a la educación primaria y a la reforma agraria. La asistencia del Banco ha sido pertinente y satisfactoria en los planos de la macroeconomía, el desarrollo del sector privado (incluidas las empresas pequeñas y medianas), el fortalecimiento del sector financiero y el desarrollo de los municipios. Sin embargo, su pertinencia y eficacia han sido desiguales en otros sectores. Los resultados de la asistencia han variado entre pertinentes y marginalmente satisfactorios en algunos sectores (abastecimiento de agua y saneamiento y transporte) y poco pertinentes o insatisfactorios en otros (salud, educación, agricultura, energía y descentralización).

Los resultados de los proyectos del Banco han sido relativamente buenos. Las calificaciones de los proyectos terminados son casi equivalentes a las de la región de Asia

FRANCAIS

transmissibles et l'accès des pauvres aux services d'éducation, ont même régressé ces dernières années.

Dans l'ensemble, les atouts l'emportent toutefois sur les handicaps. Malgré la tourmente financière qui s'est abattue sur la région, l'économie philippine se révèle davantage capable de résister et de conserver son élan que ses voisines. Le gouvernement est résolu à mener à bien et à approfondir le programme de réformes.

Au cours des douze dernières années, la Banque a recentré sa stratégie d'assistance—jusque-là axée sur le redressement économique—sur la lutte contre la pauvreté, conformément aux priorités arrêtées par le gouvernement philippin et la Banque. Ce recentrage s'est amorcé au milieu des années 90 avec le lancement de nouvelles opérations à l'appui de l'enseignement élémentaire et de la réforme agraire. L'aide de la Banque a été judicieuse et satisfaisante tant du point de vue macroéconomique qu'en ce qui concerne le développement du secteur privé (y compris les petites et moyennes entreprises, PME), le renforcement du secteur financier et le développement municipal. Elle l'a été moins dans d'autres secteurs. Ainsi, si son action a été utile et relativement satisfaisante dans certains domaines (eau et assainissement, transports), elle s'est révélée inadaptée, voire totalement inutile, dans d'autres (santé, éducation, agriculture, énergie et décentralisation).

Les projets de la Banque ont donné d'assez bons résultats. Les projets terminés ont reçu une notation pratiquement identique à celle d'opérations réalisées dans d'autres pays de la région Asie de l'Est et Pacifique (EAP) s'agissant des résultats et de la viabilité, voire meilleure pour

line with EAP averages. In early February 1998, there were but four problem projects, according to the Quality Assurance Group (QAG). The most common causes of poor performance were problems associated with project management and procurement. The overall cost of Bank assistance has been slightly above comparators' ranges because of the higher cost of supervision.

In structural adjustment, the Bank aimed to enhance the ability of the public sector to maintain macroeconomic stability and its efficiency and to improve the enabling environment for private sector development. The Bank led in the formulation and implementation of reforms in public sector management, trade and capital account liberalization, internal competition, private sector participation in infrastructure, and financial sector strengthening. It supported the reform process with a wealth of high-quality economic and sector work (ESW); effective and, on the whole, harmonious policy dialogue; good aid coordination; relevant and efficacious quick-disbursing adjustment loans; and judiciously reinforced covenants under investment projects. The strong intellectual contribution of the Bank's ESW, however, was reduced by inadequate participation and in-country dissemination, poor timing, and insensitivity to the concerns of government officials and Bank resident staff.

The institutional and economic reforms introduced with the support of the Bank since the mid-1980s, including those that restructured the central bank and strengthened the financial sector,

oriental y el Pacífico en cuanto a resultados y sostenibilidad e incluso mejores por lo que se refiere a los efectos en el desarrollo institucional. Desde mediados del decenio de 1980 todos los préstamos de ajuste (US$1.400 millones) han obtenido calificaciones satisfactorias en cuanto a sus resultados y su probable sostenibilidad. Todos menos uno han recibido una buena calificación en relación con el desarrollo institucional. Por lo que se refiere a los préstamos para proyectos de inversión (US$4.200 millones) el panorama también es positivo. Pero los resultados del Banco en la identificación, la evaluación inicial y la supervisión siguen siendo inferiores a la media de la región de Asia oriental y el Pacífico.

Los 23 proyectos de la cartera actual (US$2.200 millones) parecen estar dando resultados aún mejores: más del 90% se han calificado satisfactoriamente, un porcentaje acorde con la media de la región. Según el Grupo de garantía de calidad, a principios de febrero de 1998 sólo había cuatro proyectos problemáticos. Las causas más comunes de los resultados deficientes eran problemas relacionados con las adquisiciones y la gestión de los proyectos. El costo global de la asistencia del Banco ha sido algo superior a los de los países utilizados en la comparación, debido a unos costos de supervisión más altos.

En la esfera del ajuste estructural, el objetivo del Banco era fortalecer la capacidad del sector público para mantener la estabilidad macroeconómica y su propia eficiencia y mejorar el entorno favorable para el desarrollo del sector privado. El Banco promovió la formulación y aplicación de reformas en la gestión del sector público, la liberalización del comercio y de las cuentas de capital, la

ce qui est de l'impact du projet sur le renforcement institutionnel. Les résultats de tous les prêts d'ajustement (1,4 milliard de dollars) qui ont été menés à bien depuis le milieu des années 80 ont été jugés satisfaisants, et leur viabilité, probable. Dans tous les cas sauf un, le renforcement institutionnel a été jugé substantiel. Pour ce qui est des prêts d'investissement (4,2 milliards de dollars), le bilan est également positif. Mais la performance de la Banque du point de vue de l'identification, de l'évaluation et de la supervision des projets aux Philippines reste inférieure à la moyenne pour la région Asie de l'Est et Pacifique. Le portefeuille actuel, qui compte 23 projets (2,2 milliards de dollars) semble encore plus performant, à en croire les appréciations positives qui dépassent les 90% et rejoignent donc les moyennes pour la région. Au début de février 1998, on ne dénombrait que quatre projets à problèmes selon le Groupe de contrôle de la qualité. Les résultats décevants s'expliquent le plus souvent par des problèmes liés à la gestion des projets et à la passation des marchés. Le coût global de l'assistance de la Banque dépasse légèrement les fourchettes établies pour des projets comparables en raison du coût plus élevé de la supervision.

En matière d'ajustement structurel, la Banque s'efforce de rendre le secteur public mieux à même de maintenir la stabilité macroéconomiques et d'être efficace et de créer des conditions plus favorables au développement du secteur privé. La Banque a joué un rôle moteur dans la formulation et la mise en œuvre des réformes visant la gestion du secteur public, la libéralisation du commerce et des opérations en capital, la concurrence interne, l'ouverture du

ENGLISH

enabled the country to resist the contagion from the still unfolding East Asian crisis. The economy would have been even more resilient if the authorities had heeded the Bank's early warnings of the increasingly risky exposure to volatile short-term capital flows. Reform fatigue of the government slowed institutional and policy reforms.

To help the economy reach its growth potential, fortify its resilience to domestic and global exigencies, and reduce poverty more quickly, the government must pursue and deepen its reform agenda. While expanding its liberalized environment—a valuable distinction from its neighbors—the country must apply the lessons of the East Asian miracle as well as of the most recent East Asian crisis. Investment levels must be increased and sustained with less volatile sources of financing. Poverty must be targeted squarely, beyond the trickle-down benefits from accelerated, broad-based growth. Implementation capacity must be improved. The challenge ahead is fivefold: (i) strengthen economic management; (ii) expand private sector and infrastructure development; (iii) accelerate rural development and attack poverty aggressively; (iv) revisit human development; and (v) mobilize partnerships.

Supporting the government in pursuing this medium-term agenda should be the central feature of the Bank's assistance strategy. The Bank should move quickly beyond the immediate needs for emergency assistance to ease the current liquidity constraint. This should encompass support for a final

ESPANOL

competencia interna, la participación del sector privado en la infraestructura y el fortalecimiento del sector financiero. El Banco prestó apoyo al proceso de reforma mediante abundantes estudios económicos y sectoriales de alta calidad; un diálogo sobre políticas eficaz y, en general, armonioso; una coordinación adecuada de la ayuda; préstamos de ajuste de rápido desembolso pertinentes y eficaces, y estipulaciones prudentemente reforzadas en el marco de los proyectos de inversión. Sin embargo, la importante contribución intelectual del Banco en forma de estudios económicos y sectoriales quedó limitada por la insuficiencia de la participación y de la difusión en el país, la inoportunidad y la falta de sensibilidad ante las preocupaciones de los funcionarios estatales y del personal residente del Banco.

Las reformas institucionales y económicas que desde mediados del decenio de 1980 se han ido introduciendo con el apoyo del Banco, incluidas las de reestructuración del banco central y de fortalecimiento del sector financiero, prepararon al país para resistir el contagio de la crisis de Asia oriental, que todavía sigue extendiéndose. La resistencia de la economía habría sido aún mayor si las autoridades hubieran atendido las primeras advertencias del Banco sobre la exposición cada vez más arriesgada a corrientes muy inestables de capital a corto plazo. La fatiga reformista del Gobierno frenó la aplicación de las reformas institucionales y normativas.

Para contribuir a que la economía alcance su potencial de crecimiento, para aumentar su capacidad de resistencia frente a situaciones de emergencia a nivel nacional y mundial y para reducir la pobreza con mayor

FRANCAIS

secteur des infrastructures aux opérateurs privés et le renforcement du secteur financier. Elle a appuyé le processus de réforme en réalisant de nombreuses analyses économiques et sectorielles de qualité; en entretenant avec les pouvoirs publics un dialogue véritable et, dans l'ensemble, harmonieux sur les mesures à prendre; en assurant une bonne coordination de l'aide; en accordant des prêts d'ajustement à décaissement rapide adaptés et efficaces; et en renforçant judicieusement les dispositions contractuelles des projets d'investissement. Les analyses économiques et sectorielles de la Banque auraient cependant présenté encore plus d'intérêt si elles avaient été plus participatives et mieux diffusées sur le territoire, s'il n'y avait pas eu de problèmes de calendrier et si elles avaient davantage pris en compte les préoccupations des responsables gouvernementaux et du personnel de la mission résidente.

Les réformes institutionnelles et économique introduites avec l'appui de la Banque depuis le milieu des années 80, notamment celles qui ont abouti à la restructuration de la banque centrale et au renforcement du secteur financier, ont permis au pays de résister à la crise qui continue de sévir dans la région. Il aurait pu mieux résister encore si les autorités avaient tenu compte des mises en garde que leur avait déjà adressées la Banque sur la vulnérabilité croissante de l'économie face à la volatilité des flux de capitaux à court terme. Sous l'effet d'une certaine lassitude, le gouvernement a ralenti le rythme des réformes institutionnelles et des politiques publiques. S'il veut aider l'économie à réaliser son potentiel de croissance, à mieux résister aux

ENGLISH

phase of reforms in banking supervision and regulation, including failure resolution. Beyond this, a new compact is needed among the government, the nongovernmental organizations (NGOs), the Bank, and the rest of the donor community to mobilize and use external assistance effectively. This will require avoidance of wasteful competition among donors. The compact should support a strong medium-term development program, backed by long-term sources of foreign savings. Such an effort, which could take the form of a joint Country Assistance Strategy (CAS) with all major donors by 1999, could help the Philippines race ahead in social and economic progress.

For its part, the Bank should increase the selectivity of its nonlending assistance to improve the depth of its analysis and to increase participation. Lending assistance should be well coordinated with other donors, and larger in scale to support the unfinished reform agenda and the additional investment needs through quick-disbursing operations, financial intermediary loans, sector investment loans, guarantees, and new adaptable lending instruments.

ESPAÑOL

rapidez, el Gobierno debe aplicar y profundizar su programa de reformas. El país, al mismo tiempo que amplía su entorno liberalizado—un aspecto que lo distingue favorablemente de sus vecinos—debe tener en cuenta las experiencias derivadas del milagro de Asia oriental, así como las de la reciente crisis de esa región. Hay que aumentar los niveles de inversión y mantenerlos con fuentes de financiación menos inestables. La pobreza debe combatirse de forma directa, más allá de los efectos beneficiosos que vaya produciendo un crecimiento acelerado de base amplia. Hay que mejorar la capacidad de aplicación. El desafío para el futuro consistirá en el logro de cinco objetivos: i) fortalecer la gestión económica; ii) aumentar el desarrollo del sector privado y de la infraestructura; iii) acelerar el desarrollo rural y luchar enérgicamente contra la pobreza; iv) ocuparse nuevamente del desarrollo humano, y v) movilizar las asociaciones.

La característica central de la estrategia de asistencia del Banco debería ser el apoyo al Gobierno en la aplicación de ese programa de mediano plazo. Para aliviar los problemas de liquidez actuales es necesario que la actuación del Banco transcienda con rapidez la esfera de las necesidades inmediatas de asistencia de emergencia. Su actuación debe abarcar el apoyo a una fase final de reformas de la supervisión y la reglamentación bancarias, incluidas soluciones para los casos de quiebra. Además, es necesario un nuevo pacto entre el Gobierno, las organizaciones no gubernamentales (ONG), el Banco y el resto de la comunidad de donantes para movilizar y emplear la asistencia exterior de un modo eficaz. Para ello habrá que evitar la competencia antieconómica entre

FRANCAIS

contraintes nationales et mondiales et à réduire plus rapidement la pauvreté, le gouvernement philippin doit poursuivre et approfondir son programme de réformes. Tout en libéralisant davantage l'économie, ce en quoi il se distinguerait de bien de ses voisins, le pays doit appliquer non seulement les leçons du miracle est-asiatique, mais aussi celles de la crise qui vient de frapper la région. Il faut relever les niveaux d'investissement et les financer avec des capitaux moins instables. Il faut cibler directement la pauvreté et pas seulement compter sur les retombées d'une croissance générale accélérée. La capacité de mise en oeuvre doit être améliorée. Les défis que doit relever le pays sont au nombre de cinq. Il lui faut: i) renforcer la gestion économique; ii) promouvoir le secteur privé et développer les infrastructures; iii) accélérer le développement rural et s'attaquer énergiquement à la pauvreté; iv) repenser la valorisation des ressources humaines; et v) mobiliser les partenariats.

La stratégie d'assistance de la Banque devrait avant tout viser à aider le gouvernement philippin à poursuivre ce programme à moyen terme. L'aide d'urgence fournie par la Banque pour répondre aux besoins immédiats devrait rapidement céder la place à une assistance destinée à atténuer les contraintes de liquidités actuelles. Il s'agit d'appuyer la phase finale de la réforme de la surveillance et de la réglementation des banques, y compris le règlement des faillites. À partir de là, il faudrait en arriver à une nouvelle convention entre le gouvernement philippin, les organisations non gouvernementales (ONG), la Banque et les autres bailleurs de fonds pour mobiliser et utiliser plus efficacement

ESPANOL

donantes. El pacto debe prestar apoyo a un firme programa de desarrollo a mediano plazo, respaldado por fuentes de ahorro externo a largo plazo. Una iniciativa de ese tipo, quizá en forma de estrategia conjunta de asistencia al país para 1999 en la que participaran todos los donantes principales, podría contribuir a que Filipinas registrase un rápido progreso económico y social.

El Banco, por su parte, debe mejorar la selectividad de su asistencia no financiera para aumentar la profundidad de sus análisis y ampliar la participación. La asistencia crediticia debe estar bien coordinada con los demás donantes y alcanzar un mayor volumen para respaldar el programa inacabado de reformas y las necesidades adicionales de inversión mediante operaciones de rápido desembolso, préstamos a intermediarios financieros, préstamos para inversiones sectoriales, garantías y nuevos instrumentos de crédito adaptables.

FRANCAIS

l'assistance extérieure, ce qui permettrait d'éviter le gaspillage causé par la concurrence entre donateurs. Cette convention devrait étayer un solide programme de développement à moyen terme financé par des apports à long terme d'épargne étrangère. Un tel effort, qui pourrait prendre dès 1999 la forme d'une Stratégie d'assistance au pays (SAP) commune à tous les principaux donateurs, pourrait contribuer à accélérer le progrès économique et social aux Philippines.

Pour sa part, la Banque devrait se montrer plus sélective dans ses opérations d'aide hors prêt. Elle pourrait ainsi approfondir ses analyses et suivre une approche plus participative. Son assistance sous forme de prêts devrait être bien coordonnée avec les autres donateurs et mobiliser davantage de ressources pour financer les réformes restant à mettre en oeuvre et les besoins d'investissement supplémentaires, que ce soit par le biais d'opérations à décaissement rapide, de prêts aux intermédiaires financiers, de prêts d'investissements sectoriels, de garanties et de nouveaux instruments de prêts évolutifs.

A Tumultuous Development Decade

The Philippines has made solid economic and social progress since 1985—the last year of the economic recession coinciding with the end of the Marcos era. The succeeding Aquino and Ramos administrations have been committed to structural reform intended to trigger rapid, broad-based, sustained economic growth and social development. The Bank has provided a comprehensive package of intellectual, structural, and sectoral assistance to support those reforms, and has helped nurture country ownership of the reform program.

The country has shown its ability to deal with domestic, natural, and external crises. This resilience, commitment to reform, and the strengthened democratic institutions give grounds for hope that the Philippines will accelerate economic and social progress and emerge as a strong economic contender in the region. So far, reforms have yielded substantial results. Key economic and social indicators have improved, including poverty incidence, GNP per capita, GDP growth, life expectancy, and secondary and tertiary school enrollment. However, the government and the Bank must work closely together to secure both high, sustained economic growth and rapid poverty alleviation.

The constraints include, most notably, low levels of national savings and investment, high import duties, high population growth, a seriously strained infrastructure, an inefficient bureaucracy and judicial system, and a high incidence of communicable diseases. The poor have limited access to social services, and the quality of those services has declined.

From Crisis to Peaceful Revolution

A legacy of economic dependence on U.S. trade, capital, and aid, coupled with the concentration of wealth, land, and power in a few hundred families undermined the promise of political independence in 1946. Against a background of inefficient administration, corruption, and violence, President Marcos declared martial law in 1972. He proceeded to repress the political opposition, to centralize further an already overcentralized government, and to rely heavily on an interventionist public sector to achieve economic development. Investment rates of around 30 percent of GNP and savings rates of about 27 percent did induce rapid economic growth, but

and to improve export and investment incentives. However, the ruling elite's reluctance to loosen its control over the economy, political unrest, expansionary demand policies, a worldwide debt crisis, and the structural inability of the economy to adjust quickly to the severe external shocks of the post-1979 period (higher oil prices, an international recession, and declining export prices) precipitated a dramatic loss of investor confidence, a foreign debt moratorium, and a severe recession. Amid armed insurgencies, military defections, mounting international pressure, and a *people power revolution*, a fractious anti-Marcos coalition led by Corazon Aquino won the February 1986 elections.

The new democratic regime inherited a divided and traumatized country in deep economic crisis. Per capita output had fallen to the early 1970s levels. About 32 percent of Filipino families subsisted on incomes below the poverty line. Foreign debt service was placing a heavy burden on the limited resources the government could muster. The economy remained highly protected, with a strong anti-export bias. Private investment bottomed-out during 1985–87 at less than 14 percent of GDP. A bloated public sector contributed heavily to the fiscal deficit and to external debt. Local governments had collapsed in many parts of the country.

A Vigorous Beginning

The Aquino administration immediately launched a series of macroeconomic and structural reforms under its 1987–89 Economic Recovery Program. This sought to accelerate growth and alleviate poverty by (i) enhancing economic efficiency, (ii) reducing government intervention in productive activities in favor of private sector participation, and (iii) focusing more heavily on anti-poverty and employment-generating efforts, particularly in rural areas, and accelerating agricultural production and exports. The program called for reducing special privileges, tax exemptions, and subsidies.

In 1986 the government implemented a major reform to simplify the overall tax structure, reduce its burden on the poor, and improve collection performance. In 1988 it introduced a value-added tax to substitute for a series of sales and excise taxes that had distorted production incentives. The administration also moved (although more slowly) to liberalize trade. By the end of the 1980s, it had liberalized copra and coconut oil exports and removed import restrictions on a variety of products, including wheat, fertilizer, pesticides, textiles, chemicals, and paper products. In 1991 it intro-

distortions in the incentive framework produced inefficiencies (mainly in highly protected sectors) and slow growth in employment. Cronyism and an inward-looking development strategy perpetuated high poverty rates and inequality.

By the early 1980s, the economy, heavily dependent on imports and foreign capital, had ground to a halt. The Marcos administration had pursued some policy adjustments to liberalize trade and the financial sector,

duced a new tariff code, reducing the dispersion and the number of tariff bands and lowering overall protection in stages, with the aim of bringing the import-weighted tariff rate to 14 percent by 1995. It also removed quantitative restrictions from all nonagricultural commodities except petroleum and coal products.

At the same time, it began tackling the problems of the public enterprise sector—including heavy financial losses, duplicative functions among state-owned firms, interlocking directorates with conflicts of interest, monopolistic practices, hidden subsidies, and displacement of private investment. The government embarked on the privatization of state-owned banks and 132 nonfinancial corporations, while improving the operations of those remaining in the public sector. The privatization program proceeded slowly at the outset, mainly because of the institutional safeguards on the disposition of public assets.

The new administration moved quickly to restructure the two main government-owned banks and bring them under closer supervision. By end-1988, both banks were showing profits for the first time in several years, and one of these had been partially privatized. The government also privatized three other commercial banks. By 1989 the few remaining regulated interest rates had become market-determined.

In agriculture the Aquino administration had eliminated or reduced taxes on fertilizer and pesticides, dismantled the monopolies in sugar and coconut trading, and initiated subsector institutional reforms by 1988. It also adopted new initiatives in land reform to accelerate the transfer of land titles in rice and corn growing areas and to expand the land reform program. In 1990 Congress passed legislation to address the mounting power-generation crisis, allowing the testing of model innovative build-operate-transfer (BOT) schemes. Meanwhile, the government reconstituted a Department of Energy and made progress in depoliticizing energy price setting. Legislation passed in 1991 liberalized the environment for foreign investment.

Facing the Political Consequences of Reform

Many of President Aquino's early policies alienated key interest groups and generated strong resistance. Much of the administration's energy was devoted to investigating the sources of wealth of the former president and his associates, a goal that had some serious negative side effects, such as the closure of a 600 MW nuclear plant (a victory of the anti-nuclear lobby) without adequate

provisions for alternative power-generating capacity and the numerous legal suits that slowed down the privatization drive. Other limited resources had to be diverted for relief operations following a string of natural disasters, including typhoons, a powerful 1990 earthquake, and a major 1991 volcanic eruption. The removal of many senior and middle-level officials, coupled with a massive reorganization of the bureaucracy and layoffs following the abolishment of some departments and agencies, had reduced implementation capacity. Finally, the administration's effectiveness was undermined by weaknesses in communicating to the public about—and rallying broad support for—the goals and scope of the reforms and by the lack of an institutional mechanism for the executive and legislative branches to resolve their differences on policy reforms and spending programs.

Despite these obstacles, by the early 1990s the Aquino administration's reforms had rendered the economy among the most deregulated in the region. By 1992 the bias toward capital-intensity in investment incentives had been removed: the remaining problems (notably in tax collection, privatization, transport, agricultural trade, energy and oil, and capital markets) now became a matter of improving institutions and speeding implementation. In a notable break with the past, the private business sector and nongovernmental organizations (NGOs) became active in public affairs, and major decentralization legislation was passed in 1991.

Given these policy changes, the economic recovery was broadly based, with gross national product (GNP), gross domestic product (GDP), and the principal sectors growing steadily. Through 1989, consumption and investment grew strongly and inflation was kept at single-digit levels. Macroeconomic management in the early years of the Aquino administration was characterized by a prudent fiscal stance, conservative monetary growth, and responsible actions to reduce external debt. (This was in strong contrast to the option of unilateral selective debt repudiation that had been under discussion).[1] The country's achievements were impressive, and the growth and adjustment performance of the Philippines ranked near the top among highly indebted countries. While not as high as in some East Asian countries, growth had been relatively stable compared with that of Argentina, Brazil, and Mexico—all of which had experienced negative growth episodes. The Philippines' fiscal adjustment had been deeper and more consistent, its inflation lower and less volatile, and its external debt reduction more rapid.

Policy Weaknesses and Exogenous Shocks

Inadequacies in design and slippages in implementation of reforms seriously undermined stabilization in 1990, derailing the program agreed with the IMF and accelerating inflation during 1990–91. The agreed macroeconomic framework during 1986–89 did not call for a real devaluation, which could have stimulated export-oriented private investment. Nor did it address the worsening financial situation of the central bank, which compromised the conduct of monetary and exchange rate policy, making trade reform more difficult. Tax reform did not yield the expected revenue increases: tax administration remained weak, while the shift to a value added tax (VAT, more complex than the sales tax it replaced) was too hasty and resulted in a revenue loss. Adjustment to higher energy prices was delayed, and growing energy subsidies, uncompensated by the low-yielding tax reform, added to the consolidated fiscal deficit (which increased from 4.2 percent of GDP in 1989 to 5.5 percent in 1990) and crowded-out development-oriented public expenditures. Fiscal imbalances and a rigid exchange rate policy led to deterioration of the current account deficit from 3.4 to 6.3 percent of GDP.

Fiscal constraints on spending and institutional weaknesses retarded public investment—to 5–6 percent of GDP—and Operations and Maintenance (O&M) expenditures in priority social and economic sectors were scaled back to their real 1982 levels. Infrastructure bottlenecks worsened, particularly in power, transport, and other utilities, further discouraging private investment. A series of exogenous shocks compounded the crisis—several attempted coups (including a violent one in 1989), terms-of-trade losses, worldwide interest rate increases (partly a result of the Gulf crisis), major power shortages, an unprecedented succession of typhoons, a powerful earthquake, and a major volcanic eruption.

Under these conditions, the government had no choice but to accept what many technicians in government and at the Bank thought was an unduly restrictive program with the IMF, which was concerned about the probability of renewed slippages in the period leading up to the mid-1992 elections. Once it recommitted itself to macroeconomic discipline, however, the government succeeded in stabilizing the economy. It reduced the fiscal deficit—to 1.7 percent of GDP by 1992—in excess of program targets, although it had to accommodate major unforeseen expenditures for disaster relief. The external current account deficit fell from 6.1 percent of GDP in 1990 to 1.6 percent by 1992. However, the cost of macroeconomic tightening, political instability, and exogenous shocks was a decline in GDP of 1 percent in 1991, stagnation in 1992, and a parallel slow-down of exports.

In 1989 President Aquino expressed to Bank staff her wish not to be known merely as the "president who restored democracy," but to leave a legacy of substantial improvements in the quality of life of her people. This she did, despite the persistent efforts of dissidents in the military and the political opposition to take advantage of the population's discomfort with the social costs of adjustment and stabilization. Compared with 1985, poverty incidence was 4 percent lower in 1991, social indicators were measurably higher, GDP was 26 percent higher in 1992, and solid foundations had been laid for higher achievements in the future.

Consolidation and Revival of the Reforms

In mid-1992 the country's political landscape was still fractured. The government was battling insurgent forces from the extreme left and right and from secessionist groups in Mindanao. Natural calamities, persistent power outages, recession, and criminality had become the most pressing concerns of the electorate. General Fidel Ramos, who had been instrumental in the defense of the Aquino government against military coups, won the May 1992 elections by campaigning as a nontraditional politician and gathering support among grassroots organizations.

The tone for the new administration was set by "Philippines 2000," a long-term vision that saw the Philippines entering the twenty-first century among the ranks of the high-performing, newly industrializing countries. Economic prosperity, social equity, and political stability were the goals. Improved quality of life for every Filipino, enhanced global competitiveness, and a more participatory approach characterized the vision. The new administration recognized the need for a stable and liberalized economic environment, for openness and integration in the world economy, for private sector initiative in achieving and sustaining high growth rates, and for government innovation to complement, facilitate, and ensure a level playing field for private sector initiatives. The country's rich human resources were to be drawn into the development mainstream by employment-generating economic growth, increased investments in human capital, and varied venues for broad-based participation in planning and executing government programs. Agrarian reform remained part of the agenda. To deal with the short-term dislocations

expected to arise from structural adjustment, safety nets were to be put in place for vulnerable groups.

With broad support among the military, little debt to the traditional elites, and skillful political alliances, President Ramos engineered a smooth administrative transition, opened peace initiatives with urban insurgents and Moslem separatists, and embarked on a bold economic reform agenda in strong partnership with key legislative and civic leaders (some of whom are now presidential candidates). The administration acted to dismantle long-entrenched monopolies and cartels, as well as to prosecute serious tax evaders, bring NGOs and their agendas into the mainstream, and even oppose the Catholic Church on population policies. Poverty reduction through economic growth and social development indeed became the Ramos administration's top operational priority.

A Solid Basis for Continuing Reform

President Ramos succeeded in rallying a popular consensus behind his vision and in deepening the reforms. The government made incremental (but substantial) improve-

ments in the macroeconomic structure of the fiscal accounts (chiefly through skillful external debt management, but also through lower subsidies and a higher reliance on indirect revenues). The government completed a Brady-type debt restructuring agreement with its creditor banks in December 1992. Medium- and long-term commercial bank debt of US$4.5 billion was restructured, generating savings of around $1.5 billion and gross interest savings of around $1.8 billion over the following five years. The government continued tax reform (including the expansion of VAT in 1996), raising tax revenues from 15.3 percent in 1993 to an estimated 16.6 percent in 1997. Following a prolonged debate, Congress finally approved a new comprehensive tax reform at end-1997, aimed primarily at rationalizing the tax system, assuring its buoyancy, lowering (still rampant) tax evasion, and reducing current tax exemptions.

In the financial sector, by 1993 the administration had adopted new institutional arrangements to strengthen bank supervision and the regulatory framework, to reduce intermediation costs, and to introduce depositor protection. It successfully restructured and recapitalized the central bank, a major source of quasi-fiscal losses. Its successor is now a strong independent institution. The administration also accelerated and completed the privatization process. Both the Development Bank of the Philippines and the National Power Corporation are slated for privatization within the next few years. The still outstanding issue of how public corporations should be regulated is the subject of a Bank study under preparation.

The country made further substantial progress in trade liberalization (a highly contentious issue). In 1992 the foreign exchange market was fully deregulated for both current and capital transactions. By 1997 most quantitative restrictions had been lifted, with the important exception of rice. The share of regulated import items to the total number of tariff code lines decreased from 32 percent in 1985 to less than 3 percent in 1996. Domestic marketing and imports of petroleum products

FIGURE 1.1: REWARDING PROGRESS SINCE 1985—THE ECONOMY HAS RECOVERED

Positive Growth and Contained Inflation (Although Uneven Performance) Until the Early 1990s

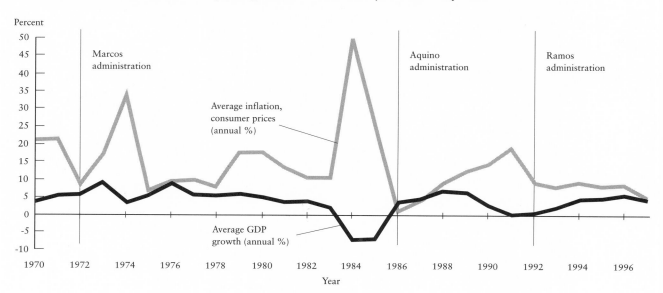

Income per Capita Has More than Doubled Since 1985, Social Indicators Have Improved, and Economic and Social Development Remain above the Regional Average

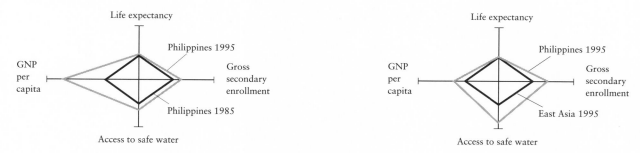

Note: The diamonds show four key indicators in the country for 1995 (in gray) compared with either its own 1985 levels or those of its neighbors for 1995.

Source: 1997 World Development Indicators, World Bank.

FIGURE 1.2: SLOW PROGRESS SINCE 1985—NEIGHBORS MADE MORE HEADWAY

National Savings, Although on the Rise, Remain Lowest within ASEAN Region

Gross National Savings (% of GNP)

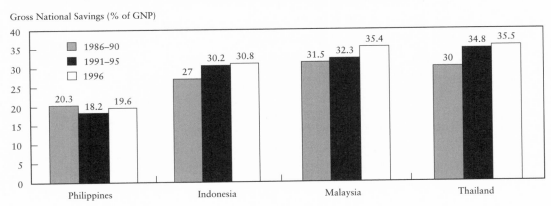

Economic Growth Performance Was Lowest within ASEAN Region

Real GDP Growth (%)

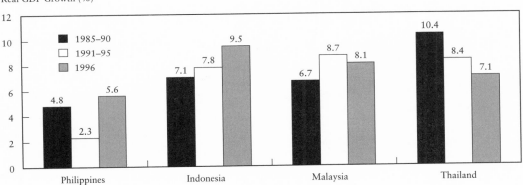

Poverty Reduction Was Substantial, but Short of East Asia's Record

Head Count Index (%)

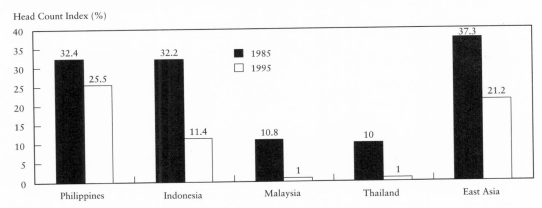

Source: World Bank and IMF staff estimates.

were fully liberalized in February 1997, but the Supreme Court struck the oil deregulation law down at end-1997, on the grounds that it did not provide a level playing field for newcomers. Congress passed a new oil deregulation law in February 1998.

With the power emergency successfully ended by 1994, the Ramos administration rationalized the BOT schemes by introducing competitive bidding and extended the BOT approach to the roads, water and sanitation sectors, and other infrastructure projects. The Philippines' BOT schemes have pioneered new forms of private sector involvement in infrastructure.

Targeted Poverty Alleviation
The government's social reform agenda (SRA), launched in September 1994, coordinates various interventions. It includes measures for access to and provision of health, nutrition, education, and shelter services for targeted groups. Twenty provinces, some with the highest incidence of poverty, have been identified under the SRA for special focus in poverty alleviation programs.

President Ramos and his key legislative allies deepened the reform agenda at a time when the economy enjoyed political stability and there was a worldwide surge of international capital to emerging markets. Reaping the benefits of stabilization and structural adjustment, macroeconomic outcomes strengthened substantially until mid-1997. In a much improved enabling environment for private sector development, the economy has responded with continued poverty reduction (another 3 percent between 1991 and 1995), accelerating growth, low inflation, and a strong currency though mid-1997.

Public sector deficits were rapidly reduced, once again beyond the targets agreed with the IMF, in the context of the June 1994 three-year Extended Financing Facility. The national government deficit shifted to a surplus in 1994, which was maintained through 1997, in spite of the slow-down in growth caused by the currency crisis. Displaying similar progress, the consolidated public sector deficit was kept below 1 percent of GNP. Output growth resumed in 1993, boosted by exports and private investment, and accelerated in the following years, reaching 5.7 percent in 1996. Private investment rose to above 21 percent of GDP, compared with less than 15 percent during 1985–88. Returning flight capital and other foreign exchange inflows nurtured reserve levels to record highs (until mid-1997).

The economic recovery was characterized by a robust expansion of foreign direct investment, which almost tripled between 1991 and 1996 (it increased more than tenfold between 1986 and 1996), and of exports, which had increased fivefold since 1985 and were still racing ahead at an annual rate of around 23 percent during 1997. End-year inflation was reduced to 6.1 percent by 1997 (since the mid-1980s, inflation had not passed 11 percent) and domestic and external debts to 58 and 48 percent of GNP by 1996 (from their peak of 85 percent and 62 percent in 1993), respectively. By 1994 the improvement in the external accounts was such that the Philippines did not require further exceptional financing from rescheduling of official debt. Total debt service due as a share of exports was reduced from above 24 percent in 1992 to below 18 percent for the medium-term. In the first half of 1997, it stood at 11 percent.

Private perceptions of economic management, institutions, and prospects improved in parallel with the liberalization of foreign investment and the trade and capital accounts, the smooth 1992 political transition, the Ramos government's strengthening of law and order, and its quick resolution of the inherited power crisis through the BOT schemes. The Brady agreement, along with macroeconomic stability and rising foreign exchange reserves, improved creditworthiness sufficiently to allow the government and some large Filipino companies to reenter international capital markets. The November 1993 price of the Philippines' new money bonds on the secondary market was 88 cents to the dollar, up from 50 cents in 1991, and well above the investment-grade threshold of 70 cents.

With the improvement in policies and institutions during the last dozen years, the country has now secured most of the conditions that have characterized the successful development path trod by its East Asian neighbors—stable but flexible macroeconomic policies, absence of major price distortions, an educated work force, an export-oriented production structure, more openness to foreign investment, limited government direct and indirect involvement in the corporate sector, and a strong banking system. These achievements give many analysts hope that the Philippines will continue to strengthen its policy framework and move up the developmental ladder.

Weathering the Storm of the Asian Crisis
Although the country has made substantial progress in four key dimensions of human development—income, poverty, life expectancy, and educational achievement—

over the past dozen years, progress has been slower than for other East Asian countries. In economic and social development, the Philippines still fares below the norm for the East Asia region. The country has regressed in some dimensions of social development, such as the incidence of communicable diseases and access by the poor to educational services of acceptable quality. It retains relatively low national savings (around 18–20 percent of GNP), low investment (22–24 percent of GNP), higher import duties (19 percent), higher population growth (2.2 percent), inadequate infrastructure, an inefficient bureaucracy and judicial system, corruption, and insecurity.

A combination of a severe, unexpected external shock—the loss of investor confidence in the sustainability of economic growth, corporate profitability, and the soundness of the region's banking system—and underlying, unaddressed structural weaknesses undermined the recent trend of accelerating growth, much as other policy weaknesses and exogenous shocks undermined economic performance during 1990–91.

East Asian economies, and the Philippines among them, certainly enjoyed too good a ride in the international financial markets. Careless investment created bubbles in the real estate, capital, and foreign exchange markets. But in the second quarter of 1997, international investors awakened to the risks involved, discovered structural economic weaknesses, and began revising their investment strategies. Because of two of its weak fundamentals—low and stagnant national savings and an appreciated real exchange rate—the Philippines was relying heavily on foreign savings to finance the large and growing gap between private investment and savings and the smaller (and shrinking) gap in the public sector. Rising dependence on short-term foreign capital inflows and loss of competitiveness left the country exposed to the contagion of the Asian financial crisis.

The foreign exchange exposure of banks and some of their prime borrowers—already a cause of concern for the regulatory authorities—had grown sharply. A sharp rise in short-term capital flows was partly misclassified in the balance of payments accounts under workers' remittances because of the component channeled through (peso conversions of) foreign currency deposit units. The loss of competitiveness had its roots in the labor market, which experienced stagnant labor productivity, and the high level of capital flows, which put downward pressure on the peso/dollar exchange rate. Monetary policy had to contend with the new concern of limiting the market-driven rise of the nominal

BOX 1.1: OVERSHOOTING ON THE WAY UP AND ON THE WAY DOWN

A recent study by senior managers of a Washington-based think-tank grouping major international banks that invest in emerging markets examined the trends in the spreads between market yields on emerging markets securities and the yields of U.S. Treasuries (the benchmark for safety). It found that the spreads accepted by international investors up to mid-1997 had narrowed more than could be explained by either the periodic upgrading by rating agencies or the improved economic fundamentals as measured by standard variables such as economic growth, inflation, and debt ratios. Overall, more than half the decline of spreads was attributable to rising global capital supply rather than improved borrowing-country fundamentals. The implication of their findings, together with current levels of the spreads, is that spreads overshot once again in the third trimester, but this time on the way up, at least for the two South Asian countries included in the econometric sample of 20 countries.

Source: Cline and Barnes, *Spreads and Risk in Emerging Market Lending*, IMF, Washington, DC, November 1997.

exchange rate, while preventing excessive monetary expansion. However, the real effective exchange rate continued to appreciate through mid-1997 (by 38 percent since 1990).

The strengthening of the peso imparted an increasing bias toward higher growth in sectors mainly producing nontradables, such as utilities and construction, holding back the potential expansion of tradable goods production, especially in the subsectors most heavily based on unskilled labor, such as textiles. Imports had risen much faster than exports and the mounting trade deficit had reached 13 percent of GNP in 1996. This pattern of growth was both unhealthy and unsustainable.

The Philippines has weathered the storm better than its neighbors, an achievement of its young economic recovery and short-lived asset bubble relative to the other Asian countries, its committed government, and limited moral hazard with respect to private investors and banks. The banking sector was in a strong position with good asset quality, competent management, and a relatively small exposure to a property sector with low vacancy rates, the result, over the last decade, of opening up the financial sector to increased foreign competition, rationalizing financial institutions, improving the regulatory environment, and the short span and limited scope of the economic boom.

In early December 1997, and in stark contrast to the downgrading of ratings for Korea, Indonesia, and Thailand, Moody once again upgraded the Philippines' debt. This was an important signal of improved confidence in the country's economic fundamentals, and in the adequacy of the response by the government to the currency crisis (and its renewed commitment to macroeconomic discipline, openness, and liberalization). But to underscore that the crisis is not over, or perhaps as another illustration of two-way overshooting, S&P has just downgraded the Philippines' long-term currency rating from stable to negative.

Fiscal balance was achieved for 1997 through a series of measures to boost tax collections and to limit current and capital expenditures. Both the extent of currency depreciation (about 37 percent in foreign currency terms) and the correction in the stock market (about 40 percent) remain less than in the other countries affected by the financial storm. No systemic problems have emerged in the banking and corporate sectors (although nonperforming loans rose from 4 percent at end-September to 5 percent reported by end-December), but the peso depreciation, brought about by the negative effect on domestic absorption, caused GDP growth rate for 1997 (at around 5.1 percent) to fall short of early projections (approaching 7 percent).

The Prospect Ahead

Despite the 1997 currency crisis and its ripple effects, the Philippines' economy is stronger now than it was a year ago. To be sure, the currency crisis is likely to cause a temporary slowdown in economic growth, with some pain for highly leveraged enterprises (and their workers) highly dependent on domestic demand. It is also possible that a few (likely small) financial institutions with weak loan portfolios and large short-term exposures in foreign currency will face bankruptcy or consolidation. The fallout on the real economy, however, is likely to be contained. Unhedged exposure to foreign liabilities by the corporate and banking sectors, accompanied by the suspected imprudent lending, was built up from only 1994 to early 1997 and, thus, did not rise to crippling levels. The government has repeatedly scaled back its growth projections for the current year to around 1.0–1.5 percent (as of September 1998) because of the continuing turmoil in global financial markets, the deepening Japanese recession, and an El Niño drought that has severely affected agricultural output. Nonetheless, the latest projection remains well above the short-term growth prospects of neighboring countries.

Over the medium term, growth is expected to benefit from the country's improved competitive position derived from depreciation of the real exchange rate. The tradable sectors will receive a boost. The export orientation of future investment will be reinforced. Paradoxically, the bursting of the bubble in the asset markets and the real exchange depreciation provides an opportunity to put long-term growth on a more sustainable policy footing. The authorities have received a strong reminder of the need to strengthen the financial sector, address the critical need to boost national savings, and correct the perverse tax and reserve incentives that favor dollar intermediation by banks through foreign currency deposits. If, as expected, the authorities will act on these signals, speculative capital flows will be discouraged in favor of longer-term portfolio and direct investments, and the banking sector will emerge strengthened and wiser.

Assistance Strategy: Satisfactory, but Uneven and Below Potential

Despite exogenous shocks, the Bank's assistance strategy over the past dozen years has been relevant and efficacious, although uneven and below potential. Throughout the period, the Bank's goals, concerns, and views were largely in tune with those of government and mainstream academia. The Bank reassessed its strategy regularly to optimize its response to the fast-changing political and economic environment, and often undertook retrospective self-evaluation. Economic recovery was the focus of Bank assistance in the late 1980s.

In the 1990s, however, poverty alleviation became the central part of the country assistance strategy, in line with the evolution of Bankwide priorities. The Bank has proved flexible enough to work effectively under sometimes trying political circumstances. Bank projects performed well. The current portfolio is at par with that of the East Asia and Pacific (EAP) Region.

Bank support for government policy reform helped usher in fundamental changes following the economic and political crisis of the mid-1980s. Untenable financial imbalances have been rectified, the country's external creditworthiness has been restored, growth has accelerated, and poverty has been reduced. The incentive framework has been strengthened, and the private sector has increasingly become the engine for export-led growth. Fundamentals in the banking sector have improved—the state has curtailed its direct involvement

in the sector, and the supervisory institutions have been strengthened. The institutional environment and public expenditure management have benefited from Bank-supported ESW, aid coordination, and lending operations. By nurturing broad public and institutional support for and ownership of the reforms, Bank assistance helped solidify their gains and strengthen their sustainability. However, Bank assistance has only a mixed record in social sector and infrastructure development because of institutional and policy constraints.

In the three years up to end-1997, with surging private capital inflows and a more confident national economic stewardship, the Bank's leverage and importance to the Philippines' economic development has decreased. The pace of policy reforms has become increasingly dictated by internal political factors. The Bank has become more open with civil society in sharing information and with its partners. In parallel, the Bank's policy dialogue has become more focused and its ESW and lending programs have become more responsive and selective.

Lower lending commitments and disbursements, and the winding-down of adjustment lending, however, represent a missed opportunity in the shape of an unfinished reform agenda, low national savings, and inadequate public investment. Both the government and the Bank should search for avenues to enhance the scale, relevance, and impact of Bank operations.

From Economic Recovery to Poverty Alleviation

In 1986 the primary objective of Bank assistance was to support economic recovery. This entailed improving public resource management to maintain macroeconomic discipline and renewing private sector confidence. A secondary objective was to improve the monitoring efforts and institutional framework for addressing poverty, particularly in rural areas. The Bank's objectives in social development were to strengthen the government's political and resource commitments to population programs, and to strengthen the institutional capacity of relevant agencies in the field.

As economic recovery and structural adjustment unfolded in the 1990s, Bank strategy became more balanced. The Bank lifted its sights to long-term growth issues such as capital market development and natural resource management. Reflecting the renewed internal prominence of its poverty alleviation mission, the strategy in 1990 called for a two-pronged approach—a reform program that would sustain economic growth, particularly with private sector initiatives, and a broad-based effort to support poverty alleviation. To support economic growth, the Bank was to provide technical advice and lending support to reinforce IMF efforts in macroeconomic management, especially in public investment monitoring and structural change. It sought to improve the enabling environment for the private sector with similar instruments through advice on—and lending for—reforms in the incentive framework for foreign investment, the regulatory framework for private sector activity, export development and diversification, ongoing deregulation (especially in transport and industry), basic infrastructure investment, and ongoing financial sector reform (particularly to develop the market for long-term finance).

In pursuit of poverty alleviation, Bank assistance sought to target three main elements—rural development (particularly infrastructure and credit facilities), family planning to reduce the high level of population growth, and human resource development. The Bank recommended that increased expenditures be directed to primary education, vocational training, urban health, nutrition, and urban infrastructure, and that the efficiency of public and private expenditures be enhanced by rationalizing and reorienting sectoral policies.

Away from the Stop-Go Syndrome

In 1993, with signs of an economic recovery under way, the Bank recognized that the country had the opportunity to break out of its stop-go growth cycles, and shifted its focus from stabilization and structural reform issues to consolidating gains, attracting private investment, and addressing emerging supply constraints in infrastructure. It called for a corresponding shift from adjustment lending to project lending, given the high levels of foreign exchange reserves and the availability of market solutions to its balance of payments problems. New lending was to focus on infrastructure, such as power, roads, water supply, and sanitation; on family planning and urban health; and on quality schooling and training. In 1994, under the *Private Sector Infrastructure Initiative,* the Bank began to address questions (including legal, regulatory, promotional, competitive, risk-unbundling, and mitigation issues) emerging from increasing private sector participation in infrastructure.

In 1995 and 1996, the Bank reaffirmed these same broad objectives, although its concerns about macroeconomic management shifted, appropriately, to issues of contingent liability management in the budget, deepening domestic capital markets, improving resiliency to potentially volatile private capital flows, and generally fostering an environment conducive to rising domestic savings. The Bank also intended to provide support for the government's social reform agenda (SRA), launched in September 1994 to provide health, nutrition, education, and shelter to targeted groups. The Bank recognized that growth needed to be supplemented with effectively targeted poverty alleviation measures. The shares of public investment in health, education, and agriculture were expected to increase sharply through 1998. With the increasing responsibilities assumed by local governments, the Bank came to pay closer attention to devolution and decentralization issues and agreed to assist in designing and implementing pilot programs of poverty alleviation in the selected priority provinces.

Over time, the Bank's attention touched virtually every area critical to long-term growth, including civil service reform (a subject of the 1995 Public Expenditure Review), housing finance, and social security reforms (beginning in 1996). With a substantially deregulated labor market, the only area of critical institutional weakness not on the Bank's radar screen during the past ten years seems to have been reform of the judicial system.

Nurturing the Reforms for Public Sector Management and Private Sector Development

A Comprehensive and Effective Package
The last quick-disbursing, policy-based Bank project, the *Economic Integration Loan* (EIL) in 1992–95, brought to an end an extended cycle of Bank support for structural adjustment in the Philippines. Since March 1987, the government has borrowed $1.2 billion to fund five major operations with complementary objectives.

These provided an appropriate continuum of lending support for the policy reform process that began under President Marcos and deepened under Presidents Aquino and Ramos. The Bank also supported structural reforms with a large body of ESW and covenant work under other investment projects.

Bank assistance covered all critical areas in public sector management, trade and capital account liberalization, internal competition, private sector participation in infrastructure, and financial sector strengthening. The EIL extended and deepened the sequence of economic reforms, as in the process of tariff reform and import liberalization that had been included in earlier Bank operations—*Structural Adjustment Loans I* and *II*, the *Agriculture Sector/Inputs Loan*, and the *Economic Recovery Loan* (ERL, which also supported a major tax reform). Similarly, while the government's financial

---

BOX 2.1: EXPERIENCES OF FIAS AND MIGA

The Foreign Investment Advisory Service (FIAS), a joint agency of the International Finance Corporation (IFC) and the World Bank, has been active in the Philippines for almost ten years, completing a range of projects relating to both the policy environment and promotion strategies. In 1988 it prepared a study of how policy and institutional change could stimulate investment in agribusiness. FIAS also helped the central bank to review its debt-to-equity swap program in 1989. The most recent projects completed were advice on the formulation of a National Investment Promotion

Plan (FY96) and assistance with refining the regulations for BOT projects (FY97). Currently FIAS is preparing to undertake a review (cofinanced by AusAID) of the impediments to foreign direct investment (FDI) in Mindanao. The project will also examine the existing capacity of the provincial governments to carry out effective investment promotion activities.

Multilateral Investment Guarantee Agency (MIGA) staff have visited the country regularly, about once a year. In spite of these promotional activities, there has been low demand for MIGA's services from the Philippines. Only two contracts

of guarantees in the Philippines for a maximum outstanding liability of US$60 million in the banking and power sectors (Internationale Nederlanden Bank, N.V., and Magma Netherlands, B.V.) have been issued. MIGA has over 20 preliminary applications outstanding for guarantee in the oil and gas, mining, and power sectors, totaling US$1.8 billion in proposed investment. The Region has not requested any substantial input from MIGA in past Country Assistance Strategies (CASs), economic work, or policy dialogue. The reasons for the low demand for MIGA services from

prospective investors in the Philippines are unclear, but perceived political risk, economic instability, and the availability of cheaper coverage elsewhere could be explanatory factors. MIGA's outstanding liabilities are far from past or current per-country coverage ceilings. However, this is not out of line with other countries, being about 25 percent and 80 percent of MIGA's exposure to Pakistan ($160 million) and Indonesia ($76 million), respectively. The recent currency crisis may well bring more applications to MIGA from all over the East Asia region, including the Philippines.

Source: FIAS and MIGA.

institutions were restructured under the ERL, financial restructuring of the central bank was supported by conditionality added to the second tranche of the *Financial Sector Adjustment Loan* (FSAL, 1989–92), and concurrently by the EIL.

The *Reform of Government Corporations Loan* (RGCL, 1988–92) supported the government privatization program, focusing on the critical institutional arrangements necessary for the sale or divestiture of government-owned corporations and the adoption of a framework for improving the functioning of corporations that would remain in the public sector. Conditionality in this area was extended further by the EIL. The *Debt Management Loan* (DML, 1990–92) supported a first-phase debt and debt-service reduction agreement with commercial banks (the first such operation supported by the Bank). The second and final stage of the commercial bank debt reduction program, completed in December 1992, was considered a key part of the EIL. This project was important in reestablishing international confidence in the Philippines.

BOX 2.2: IFC'S ROLES AND STRATEGIES FOR PRIVATE SECTOR DEVELOPMENT

The IFC has been active in the Philippines for three and a half decades, and its operations have inevitably reflected the changing business environment. It has supported the development of the financial sector; facilitated and encouraged the entry of other investors, especially in private infrastructure; and demonstrated, through the success of projects in which it has made investments, profitable new business opportunities for project sponsors. Since 1963 the IFC has approved US$1.84 billion in financing, including US$1.0 billion for its own account, for 79 investments in the Philippines with a total project cost of US$8.4 billion. The IFC's current committed and disbursed portfolio contains 20 projects with IFC financing of US$266 million.

Source: IFC.

In the 1970s, because of easier access to foreign currency credits for Philippine businesses, and later because of the increasing role of government, the IFC's operations went through a change in emphasis from financing the expansions of large established companies, such as the dominant telephone and electricity utility, to investing in medium-size enterprises such as mining, chemicals, and agribusiness. To facilitate investments in the region, the IFC established the regional office for East Asia and the Pacific, one of the first field offices in Manila, in 1977. In the early 1980s the adverse economic situation seriously affected many firms. During this period, projects were held back, and the IFC tried to reach out to companies with smaller and more immediate financing

needs. The IFC helped to finance All Asia Capital, which has since become the second-largest non-bank finance company in the Philippines.

In the second half of the decade, a set of new policies provided an improved environment for development of the private sector, which was, however, still constrained by lack of access to foreign capital. The IFC provided funding to several agribusinesses, to manufacturing projects, and to two major hotel projects. It resumed lending to the telephone utility and to the reprivatized Meralco, again to fund their foreign-currency-denominated capital expenditures. To help small and medium enterprises, IFC made an equity investment in a venture capital fund, provided a credit line to All Asia Capital, and separately made

equity investments in four medium-size companies under this program. The growing electricity crisis raised new challenges. The turning point came with the introduction of BOT contracts for the construction of new power plants. The IFC made the pioneering investment in Hopewell Energy (Phil.) for the country's first independent private power project. IFC financial participation provided sponsors and other institutions with the required comfort to make significant long-term commitments.

With improved political stability and a more favorable macroeconomic environment after 1992, the economy moved to a faster growth track. The IFC provided funding for additional power projects—in all, helping to finance over 2,200 MW

Against heavy odds, the Aquino administration made substantial progress in structural adjustment. Its efforts were supported by four major Bank loans—the ERL ($300 million), the RGCL ($200 million), the DML ($200 million), and the FSAL ($300 million). These loans yielded mixed and gradual results. Their true value was in getting the structural reform ball rolling, which yielded substantial results once political and fiscal stability became increasingly secure after 1991–92.

After the Philippines returned to macroeconomic discipline in 1991, the Bank continued its support with tranche releases from the three ongoing adjustment operations (FSAL, RGCL, and DML). A new operation—the EIL ($200 million)—sought to complete the original reform agenda by assuring sustained improvements in macroeconomic management and the environment for private investment. Its specific objectives were to strengthen the finances of the central bank, set appropriate energy pricing policies, continue to deepen trade liberalization, promote liberalization in the transport

of additional capacity in the Philippines. These early projects helped the country address the problem of power shortages, and had an important demonstration effect and provided a model for further investments in power and other infrastructure projects, using the BOT and related contractual arrangements. The IFC also provided funding for the expansion of cement and oil refining capacities, needed for the growing economy. In addition, IFC invested in several venture capital funds to help small and medium enterprises (SMEs) in the construction materials and infrastructure sectors and provided start-up capital for companies in emerging fields such as semiconductors and computer software.

For about three years until the regional currency crisis in mid-1997, the increased confidence of investors in the Philippines, as well as the liberalization of the financial sector, made it easier for established companies to gain access to funds on both domestic and international markets. This reduced the need for IFC funding for established companies, and its investments declined significantly in FY95 and FY96. The IFC refocused its strategy to emphasize regional development, SMEs, complex infrastructure projects requiring longer-term funding, and privatization services. In FY97, the IFC invested in a newly licensed telephone company, a shipping line, and a greenfield petrochemical project and arranged a long-term credit line aimed at infrastructure projects for a local bank. The IFC also provided advisory services for the successful privatization of Metropolitan Waterworks and Sewerage System (MWSS), Asia's largest water sector privatization, which has already delivered private sector efficiencies in the form of significantly lower prices. Over the next few years, water supply will be upgraded and extended to cover 3.5 million previously unserved residents of Metro Manila. The estimated US$7 billion cost of these improvements will now be funded by private investors.

Following the currency crisis, the IFC plans to focus even more on the financial sector. It is looking for ways to support further deepening and strengthening of the financial sector by helping to establish a new credit-rating agency and through investments in leasing, housing finance, factoring, and the mutual fund industry. Given the recent increase in interest rates and the decline in equity markets, the IFC is also working with established companies to help them increase access and diversify their sources of long-term funds. The IFC is looking to help finance health care and education in the Philippines, using its recent experience in other countries in the region. In addition, it has initiated and helped in arranging funds for studies on microcredit and SMEs, along with sector studies on tourism and fisheries, focused on the less-developed southern islands. These and other studies by FIAS will help the overall development of the private sector and further help IFC to formulate its own strategy for how best to support the private sector and development in the Philippines.

sector, open the economy to foreign investment, complete the government's' privatization program, and liberalize the foreign currency market.

The EIL was highly successful. The loan achieved or exceeded all its immediate targets and its broader development goals. The government restructured the central bank and brought the Oil Price Stabilization Fund into surplus, correcting a key source of the persistent fiscal deficit in previous years. It made impressive gains in liberalizing the foreign exchange regime. It recognized the hitherto informal liberalized entry and fare-setting practices in the transport sector. New legislation opened most sectors to foreign ownership, increasing foreign investment considerably. The government reduced the debt of commercial banks and its debt services (helping external creditworthiness), privatized more than 100 government corporations, reduced import tariffs, eliminated most quantitative restrictions (with the nagging exception of agricultural products), and promoted a more competitive environment. Notwithstanding delays in the privatization and energy-pricing initiatives and final compromises about agricultural quantitative restrictions, the Bank has supported substantial economic strengthening and has helped the government to establish a track record of sound macroeconomic management since 1992.

The Bank and OED Warned about Macroeconomic Weaknesses

Up until the end of 1996, international investors had rushed to shower the Southeast Asian economies with huge and mounting capital flows; they then rushed out, pulling along domestic investors. But the IMF, the Bank, and OED did not neglect to alert the authorities to the risks imposed by the country's weaknesses in the face of this volatile investment environment. They issued repeated warnings, beginning in 1994—including one by the Bank's Regional vice-president in 1995—about the low level of domestic savings, the appreciating real exchange rate and rising trade deficit, and the mounting exposure to short-term capital inflows.

The June 1995 OED audit of the *Debt Management Loan* had warned that encouraging large short-term capital inflows was not a good objective. Evidence was already visible that the increased capital inflows of the 1990s had brought about some complacency about serious macroeconomic problems. In the 1994 *Country Economic Memorandum,* the Bank analyzed the problems of low investment and savings levels, and of inter-national competitiveness (including factors brought about by the appreciating real exchange rate). The 1996 *Financial Sector Assessment* mission highlighted the risks to the financial sector, including those from rising exposure to real estate, the stock market, and foreign exchange. The government heeded only some of these recommendations, postponing action on others until after "exiting" from the IMF program. All this was partly a matter of complacency and partly a matter of "reform fatigue" among politicians.

All concerned knew that excessive capital inflows can become destabilizing, and the Philippines had direct experience of that as a consequence of the Mexican crisis in the first half of the 1990s. Here too, the government only partially heeded the full lessons from the crisis—presented to the government by the Bank in a June 1995 informal policy note. The Bank had indeed warned that a sudden shift in investor sentiment could quickly drain the Philippines' $6–7 billion reserves and cautioned that early market signals should be monitored closely.

The Bank did recommend that tight fiscal and financial management be maintained; that foreign exchange reserves not be squandered to resist a market-driven exchange rate adjustment, except for intervention to smooth excessive day-to-day volatility; that the government not experiment by issuing debt linked to or denominated in foreign currency (which it did, with various bond issues that established a benchmark and facilitated private sector access to the international capital markets; see Statistical Annex Table 5.1); and that the government consider a temporary capital inflow tax that would penalize short-term flows (as in Brazil) to avoid the risk of overdependence on private short-term capital in financing the current account (no action was taken to discourage short-term capital inflows); that the authorities monitor, supervise, and keep under control the foreign exchange exposure of the government, government-owned and controlled corporations (GOCCs), and financial institutions; and that government undertake more aggressive intervention to buy foreign exchange to avoid upward pressure on the peso not justified by economic fundamentals, balanced by a tighter fiscal policy to preserve monetary targets and to affect the current account directly (instead, the real exchange rate was allowed to appreciate by 17 percent between 1994 and July 1997).

However, all analysts within and outside the Bank were caught by surprise in mid-1997 by the extent of the crisis of confidence that led to the rapid depreciation of the peso. Indeed, the strong yet short-lived macroeconomic expansion of the mid-1990s, the rapid progress toward a more market-oriented economy, the good export performance, and the large net capital inflows long dampened fears that the (recognized) macroeconomic weaknesses posed a serious risk to growth and currency stability in the short run.

Sectoral Assistance: An Uneven Performance

Strengthening the Financial Sector. At the end of 1986, the Philippines had 29 commercial banks. Four were foreign-owned, one was government-owned, and the remainder were generally small and family-controlled indigenous banks with high operational costs. As of September 1997, there were 52 commercial banks—all but 3 privately owned, and 17 under foreign ownership. Of

these, 5 are engaged in derivative trading, and 17 may also invest in and underwrite equities. Three specialized government financial institutions remain, the Development Bank of the Philippines, the Land Bank, Al Amanah Bank, in addition to the National Housing Mortgage Finance Corporation.

The growth and shift in configuration of the banking sector shows the effectiveness of government policy reform in opening up the sector, and of the Bank's package of assistance, designed to build on the significant deregulation implemented during the 1980s. The Bank provided its support with an appropriate mix of policy-based sectoral adjustment and investment operations, well-grounded in prior ESW. Most of this was undertaken with the endorsement of the government, and the Bank endeavored to ensure, especially in the 1990s, that

---

BOX 2.3: MICROCREDIT LESSONS BY THE ASIAN DEVELOPMENT BANK

The Asian Development Bank (ADB) approved a US$8 million loan for microcredit in 1988. This was the first microcredit program aimed at providing credit to cottage enterprises in rural areas. The loan was disbursed through the Department of Trade and Industry's network of NGOs: 312 NGOs participated in disbursing loans to 21,000 sub-borrowers, who generated 46,000 jobs at around US$200 each. The loan was disbursed 15 months in advance, and it was rated as successful.

According to the ADB, the program, despite its lack of emphasis on group lending as

used by the Grameen Bank, "has enjoyed an astonishing 86 percent repayment rate, which, when late payment is counted, soars to 99 percent." One-quarter of the program's independent entrepreneurs—most of them under the poverty line—have graduated to become bankable SMEs. The ADB is not only using credit to reduce poverty, but it is also helping "to build a middle class so important to Asia's growing economies." A second loan for US$31 million has already been disbursed, and, as of 1996, the NGO II loan had generated 190,000 jobs among 100,000 microenterprises.

In contrast, the World Bank approved a US$15 million loan for microlending in 1989. The project closed one year ahead of time in 1993, and 90 percent of the loan was canceled. The loan was retailed by commercial banks through the Development Bank of the Philippines. The project aimed at substituting collateral through mutual guarantee associations that grouped potential borrowers and provided guarantees for loans made to their members. Individual contributions of US$400 to the association made members eligible for a loan of up to US$3,600.

However, neither the

commercial banks nor the individual borrowers were much interested in the new associations. Commercial banks did not consider the associations attractive clients. Only 39 associations were established, and the number of members per association had to be reduced from 60 to 40 to make smaller associations eligible for the loan. The 1996 OED audit of the project found that "the main lesson of the project is that an untested approach for lending to microenterprises should not be adopted on a national scale without first trying a pilot operation . . . to test the feasibility of the scheme."

Source: *Asian Business* (December 1996) and OED Précis No. 135 (January 1997).

all major stakeholders retained ownership of ESW-based reform. One notable exception—an example of the sometimes testing relationship between the Bank and the government—was the 1996 *Financial Sector Assessment* study. Despite a solid review of urgent financial issues and concrete, relevant policy recommendations, Bank staff undertook the assessment over the objections of both the central bank's governor and the Bank resident representative about its timing and modalities. This disagreement led to a distancing of the Bank from active involvement in banking sector reform.

Nevertheless, the overall effect of the Bank's assistance to the financial sector has been highly satisfactory. Domestic financial markets have become considerably stronger, deeper, and more deregulated since the wrenching crisis of the mid-1980s. The ratio of broad money (inclusive of foreign currency deposits) to GNP has since more than doubled, while loan portfolios have remained relatively healthy. Reforms supported by the FSAL enabled the strengthened central bank and the Philippines' financial system to cope effectively with the aftershocks of the Mexican crisis in 1994 and 1995 and with the recent and more severe Asian crisis. In retrospect, the FSAL may be considered one of the most successful of the Bank's financial sector operations. With the Bank, the government deserves considerable credit for its strong commitment, decisive action, and exemplary leadership.

But financial deepening and strengthening in the Philippines still has some way to go. Its broad money-to-GNP ratio of 52 percent in 1996 is still low in comparison with Malaysia (at 95 percent) and Thailand (at 81 percent). And the sector still suffers from weaknesses in the regulatory and supervisory regime—the absence of risk-weighted capital adequacy and of prudential regulations, and a lag in supervisors' technical ability to assess with rigor the recently introduced, complex financial derivatives. The banking secrecy laws, personal liability of supervisory officials, and cumbersome legal/judicial procedures constrain enforcement.

Modest Assistance to SMEs. Between 1976 and 1992, the Bank provided US$180 million to finance SMEs through four consecutive lines of credit. The ADB contributed US$100 million to the last line of credit. All four lines of credit were retailed as subloans to eligible SMEs. Over that period, the Bank financed almost 2,600 subprojects, which generated around 64,000 jobs. Besides channeling credit to SMEs, the Bank also supported a number of nonlending activities affecting SMEs, directly and indirectly, such as the overall policy dialogue with the government, SME-specific economic and sector work, and direct technical assistance to SMEs.

The Bank's SME strategy had two major objectives. First, the Bank sought to increase the availability of long-term funds to SMEs directly through the participation of financial institutions. Second, the Bank sought to generate jobs (especially outside Manila), which would ultimately reduce poverty. Cumulatively, the SME projects were an effective credit allocation program, but modest in job-generating capacity. These projects yielded satisfactory outcome ratings in the increased availability of long-term funds (market rates were obtained) and creation of jobs, but made only a small dent in the aggregate unemployment picture and in reducing poverty.

Poor Result-Orientation of Social Sector Projects. The Bank's strategy to alleviate poverty did not translate into concrete action on the ground in the social sectors until recently. In general, supervision missions have focused on disbursing funds and obtaining compliance with specific loan covenants. Until recently, relatively little attention was devoted to actual accomplishments in the field. The Bank's subsector-specific lending has yielded contrasting results—progress on key indicators of social development, but regression in some areas.

Bank Assistance for Health: No Measurable Impact. The recorded improvements in health indicators and the (modest) reduction of the population growth rate to the mid-1990s cannot be credited to Bank activities. Since the late 1980s, the Bank has stepped-up its direct lending support for priority areas (reproductive health, primary care, and disease control) and has been the main coordinator of donors in the sector. But its lending assistance has remained modest, mainly because of the govern-

ment's preference for concessional donor financing. Only one project has been completed, and it has not yet been evaluated. Consequently, it is not possible to assess the impact of the Bank's assistance on health indicators. On the positive side, the Bank has pushed successfully for efforts to control malaria and tuberculosis. On the negative side, broad input indicators—such as O&M expenditures and public investment in the sector—have remained minuscule (and inadequate), as in the preceding 15 years. With the added leverage of structural adjustment lending, the Bank could certainly have done more in health, especially in pushing for a change in resource allocation and in policies related to hospital utilization.

A 1991 Bank study, *New Directions in the Philippines Family Planning Program*, contributed to the government's substitution of a new "health" rationale for family planning in place of the old and ineffective "population growth reduction" approach. It also provided an appropriate agenda, focused on reproductive health, for Bank lending for family planning. This agenda was indeed reflected in the *Women's Health and Safety* project (1995), but the government's advocacy, leadership, and institutions remain too weak for the family planning program to have substantial influence against the strong opposition by the Catholic Church.

Bank Assistance in Education: A Mixed Impact. Although the Bank has supported textbook production, in-service teacher training, and the development of subject curricula, overall project performance and institutional achievements have been disappointing. The reallocation and expansion of budgetary expenditures in favor of the education sector has also been unsuccessful. And although enrollment rates have increased, the quality of education and access to services for students from poor families have not improved.

The Bank's current emphasis on the quality of elementary education and its accessibility to students from poor families serves its poverty alleviation objectives well. Its secondary emphasis on improving vocational and technical training to meet the needs of an expanding economy appears less justified. Little evidence is available that the Bank has identified the market failures that would justify government involvement. The quality of these projects at entry is highly unsatisfactory.

The most recent loan, the *Third Elementary Education* project, addresses areas of weakness with a high-risk, high-reward approach. It seeks to replace the centralized educational system with a decentralized mechanism, involving greater participation by stakeholders, including parents' associations, local communities, and NGOs. It specifically targets poor provinces and disadvantaged children and is introducing the use of in-service training and grant mechanisms to promote school-based improvements in management and innovative approaches to education. The project intends to improve institutional capacity so that the relevant agencies can effectively implement their strategy. Coverage is limited to the 20 provinces targeted by the Social Reform Agenda (SRA), plus 6 other poor provinces. Supervision ratings indicate that project start-up has proceeded well—but caution is warranted, given the ambition of the effort and sector experience.

Adequate Attention to Gender. Improvements in gender equality in public policy have been made during the past dozen years. Women's legal status, although already high by international standards, improved further. But problems in reproductive health (high total fertility, maternal mortality, and morbidity rates) and the labor market (gender gap in labor force participation rate, wages, and unemployment rate) have persisted. The Bank's focus on the reproductive health issue appears warranted. Consultation and communication with government agencies, women's NGOs, and donors with gender-related programs need to be intensified.

Limited Impact for Bank Assistance in Many Other Sectors. Government policy reform, expenditures, and Bank support for the basics of the economy—agriculture, natural resource management, energy, transport, and water and sanitation—have yielded little in the way of substantive outcomes. The government and the Bank can claim success only in two sectors—water and sanitation and municipal development—but even these are qualified successes. A variety of problems have thwarted more effective and supportive development throughout the core economic sectors—a dearth of institutional capacity, project implementation delays, unresolved policy issues, and poorly timed Bank support. The Bank certainly overestimated the development learning curve of the new Aquino administration. Most development programs in the late 1980s were plagued with budgetary and procurement problems.

In *agriculture*, the Bank's track record of assistance is less than satisfactory.[1] In the implementation of its strategy, the Bank's priorities included fostering agricultural growth, but without adequate emphasis for the equity dimensions of such growth, or for land reform or the targeting of projects to assure rapid poverty reduction. The

National Irrigation Authority, which the Bank had helped build into one of the most effective irrigation institutions in the developing countries in the 1970s and early 1980s, had deteriorated by the late 1980s. So far, there has been no effort to support product diversification strategies, except for some indirect support through the rural credit projects. The Bank's reform efforts in the sector, which had a good start in the mid-1980s, have failed to prevent serious backsliding in trade liberalization.

On the positive side, Bank assistance for irrigation helped the Philippines achieve self-sufficiency in rice production. The areas with irrigation systems financed under the Bank's programs have the lowest incidence of rural poverty. In agricultural education and technology transfer, the Bank helped finance the development of a renowned international center for agricultural education. The Bank also helped capitalize on the green revolution.

Yet growth in the sector remains disappointing. Poverty in rural areas has declined slowly, and less so than in urban areas. Institutional capacity among sectoral agencies remains weak at both the national and the local government levels. After more than three decades of lending and policy advice, there is no sign that the sector is on the road to sustained recovery. However, a recent study, *Promoting Equitable Rural Growth* (1997), outlines a new comprehensive strategy for rural development.

In *environmental management*, the adoption of the *Philippine Strategy for Sustainable Development* in 1989 has not yet addressed the factors that threaten environmental sustainability. The Bank's pioneering environmental work in the Philippines laid the foundations for a program of donor support for environmental reform, with extensive NGO participation. The *Central Visayas Regional* project innovations related to upland tenure were important catalysts for the adoption of the 25-year lease under the Social Forestry Program that became a centerpiece of the Aquino administration's environmental policy. The Bank has adequately integrated environmental management concerns in its strategy and has correctly diagnosed the conditions that would allay resource degradation and ease serious environmental stress. However, it has not moved forcefully beyond that stage. Its project work is rated as satisfactory, because it has pushed the government in the right environmental direction—at least to an abiding awareness of its slowly deteriorating environment. But that effort has taken a long time, and has not yet yielded substantive results.

In *energy*, Bank assistance since 1986 has not been successful, although performance of all but one completed Bank project has been rated as satisfactory. For the *Energy Sector Loan* approved in 1990, however, a draft OED audit is proposing to rate outcome as marginally unsatisfactory, sustainability as uncertain, and institutional development impact as modest. The government, its own National Power Corporation (NPC), and the Bank all failed to anticipate the disastrous implications for power supplies of the mothballing of the half-completed 600 MW nuclear power plant and the lack of planning and alternative investment. Moreover, Bank input into the design and implementation of the government's BOT initiative, which effectively solved the severe power shortages of the early 1990s by 1994, was minimal. At best the Bank was unenthusiastic, at worst it opposed the program out of concern for its high direct cost. In neither case did the Bank adequately appreciate the high cost of inaction.[2] The IFC, however, made a pioneering investment in the first arrangement, thus offering its partners the comfort to make long-term commitments and providing a model for subsequent arrangements (see Box 2.3). Compared with the early 1990s, consumers today are undoubtedly better-served, but transmission bottlenecks persist, and the quasi-governmental distribution sector (which has unacceptably high technical and nontechnical losses) continues to suffer from underinvestment.

The Bank's efforts at restructuring NPC since 1991 have not yielded sustained results. The Bank has lent nearly a billion dollars to a noncreditworthy NPC over the past decade, but NPC's estimated 1997 internal cash-generation was still negative, in contravention of loan covenants. The recent peso depreciation, unaccompanied by adequate tariff adjustments, has further increased NPC's losses. Because of NPC's continuing financial troubles, several large, recently commissioned, and privately financed power plants will sit idle for long periods, pending completion of the transmission lines (Bank-financed) by NPC. Other Bank-financed plants affected by lack of transmission lines are expected to resume production after March 31.

The Bank has highlighted the right issues in the sector dialogue, particularly those relating to energy pricing, power sector restructuring, and oil sector deregulation. In 1992 the Bank extended a Policy and Human Resources Development Fund (PHRD) grant for technical assistance to support NPC's preparation for privatization. This should yield positive results soon

after the May presidential elections, as passage is expected of the Omnibus Bill, which would allow the privatization of NPC and would complete the regulatory framework for private participation, including tariff setting. Supervision ratings depicted all five projects in the Bank's active portfolio during 1997 as satisfactory performers, but caution is warranted: all were rated unsatisfactory for quality at entry, and one (the *Rural Electrification* project) is now suffering from serious implementation delays.

In *water and sanitation*, the Bank has extended 10 loans totaling US$540 million since the late 1970s. Concluding in the early 1980s that the Local Water Utilities Administration (LWUA) was not a suitable borrower, yet wishing to support the sector and development in provincial areas, the Bank made loans to the Metropolitan Waterworks and Sewerage System (MWSS), serving Manila, and a nationwide sector loan in 1990 for water supply and sanitation, relying on three government departments and local governments as implementing agencies.

The Bank's completed lending operations for water supply and sanitation have had mixed results and are rated as only marginally satisfactory. Under the projects, some physical targets were met (for example, distribution extensions), others (service coverage and reduction of unaccounted-for water) were not. Projects were invariably completed several years behind schedule because of delays in procurement, poorly performing contractors, and shortages of local funds. Despite significant accomplishments, which kept the Philippines ahead of most other Southeast Asian countries (except Malaysia), some 35 percent of the 28 million residents in large urban areas do not have piped water, and most have no satisfactory way of disposing of waste; the situation in rural areas is worse. But the Bank's substantial efforts at policy review in the 1990s, its decision to forgo substantial lending opportunities rather than channel funds though an unreformed LWUA, and its recent approach in the sector—bottom-up planning and local government participation—may help improve the portfolio's performance.

In *municipal development*, several lending operations in urban infrastructure have adapted to the reality of local governments and have become useful tools in decentralization efforts. Since the mid-1980s, municipal development loans have become effective mechanisms to finance local programs and open the doors of creditworthy local governments to the domestic credit markets through the Municipal Development Fund (a fourth line of credit is in the pipeline).

However, in *decentralization* policy, analytical work to provide in-depth advice to the country was not completed as planned and achieved only partial results. The Bank started planning an analysis of local government finance in June 1988. But the resulting study, *Fiscal Decentralization,* was released in early 1993, when most of the key issues had already been settled and parliament had already adopted final changes to the local government code. The government has preferred to tap other donors for analytical work in recent years. However, a 1996 Bank policy note and two 1994–97 studies financed with IDF grants helped prepare a policy framework for financing local investments that has been adopted by the donor community. We should note that consideration of long-standing Bank recommendations regarding the introduction of equalization criteria in the allocation of national revenues and of incentives for local revenue mobilization have been postponed until after the coming elections.

In *transport,* the Bank's strategy has been ambitious and has focused on the removal of three constraints—financial, institutional, and policy—with mixed results. The Bank has supported deregulation, private sector participation, institution-building, and higher O&M expenditures. Lending operations have focused on the key road subsector. From 1985 to the present, seven transport projects—including one structural adjustment operation with a substantial transport reform component—were under implementation (five were completed and two are ongoing). The *Maritime Improvement* project, which has been under preparation since 1992, was canceled in 1997 because of disagreement with the government on its policy content. Coordination with other donors—in project and sector work—was good.

The deregulation that the *Economic Integration Loan* supported was largely an acceptance and legalization of existing conditions. And the impressive initial gains made in private involvement in the road and port subsectors have been rolled back. For instance, private sector participation in road maintenance increased from 10 percent in 1984 to 70 percent in 1994, but was then forced down to 50 percent through political interference. The most important objective of Bank assistance, maintenance of the road system, has been undermined by insufficient budgetary allocations (about 0.2–0.3 percent of GNP in recent years for the transport and communications sectors).

Instruments and Partnership

High-Quality Economic and Sector Work, but with Missteps

The Bank's diagnosis of the Philippines' ills has been correct and based on solid economic and sector work (ESW)—at both the macro and the sectoral levels. The government has valued the Bank's intellectual contributions, embodied in consistently high-quality reports covering all key areas. Country economic memorandums and public expenditure reviews, drawing from many other internal and external studies and policy papers, have contributed to developing the broad reform agenda. Informal policy notes, summarizing the Bank's views on specific issues or drawing lessons from the Bank's worldwide experience, have facilitated policy dialogue. The donor community has also benefited from this work.

But problems with dissemination and timing have limited ESW effectiveness and impact. Key middle and senior managers in government, parliamentary committee chairmen, business leaders, former cabinet members, and prominent intellectuals are frequently unaware of the content (and sometimes even of the existence) of nonsensitive Bank reports (for example, the 1994 *Public Expenditure Review,* a very expensive report, had only a modest impact on the allocation of expenditures). In some cases, the country arrived at strategic or legal decisions before the Bank was able to complete work on its reports (as in the case of the Bank's 1993 *Fiscal Decentralization Study*). Similarly, the 1996 *A Strategy to*

FIGURE 2.1: COMPARATIVE OED EVALUATION FINDINGS BY FISCAL YEAR OF APPROVAL (US$ MILLION)

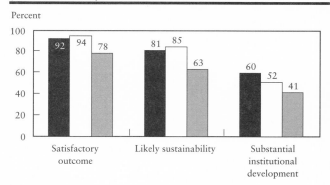

Percent

Philippines: Satisfactory outcome 92, Likely sustainability 81, Substantial institutional development 60
East Asia and Pacific Region: Satisfactory outcome 94, Likely sustainability 85, Substantial institutional development 52
Bankwide: Satisfactory outcome 78, Likely sustainability 63, Substantial institutional development 41

■ Philippines
□ East Asia and Pacific Region
▨ Bankwide

Fight Poverty proved poorly timed, given the extensive work already conducted under the umbrella of a presidential commission in preparation for a poverty summit.[3] The 1996 *Financial Sector Assessment* failed to account adequately for the sensitivities of the authorities. The Bank fell short in providing adequate technical and policy reform analysis in an area critical for the social and economic reform agenda—the judicial system's institutional weaknesses—and in exploring gender discrimination issues in the labor market.

Sound Project Lending Performance

In the twelve years from FY86 to FY97, the total annual direct cost of delivering the Philippines' country program (lending and nonlending services) has ranged between US$5.5 million and US$7.6 million (in constant FY97 dollars), FY97 being the lowest cost, and FY91 the highest. Total costs in staff time have ranged between 31 and 34 staffyears. In the same period, the Bank approved 49 projects to the Philippines, totaling nearly US$5.7 billion. Of this amount, about 74 percent (US$4.2 billion as of February 1998) has been disbursed. About 25 percent of commitments (US$1.4 billion) have gone to adjustment lending, and 75 percent (US$4.2 billion) to investment lending. Adjustment lending was concentrated in the 1987–93 period. It was halted after FY93.

Overall Relevance and Efficacy. Bank assistance has been both relevant and satisfactory at the macro level, and in private sector development (including SME lending), financial sector strengthening, and municipal devel-

---

opment, using a variety of instruments—adjustment loans and policy dialogue, specific investment loans for financial intermediaries and local infrastructure, aid coordination, and technical assistance. The Bank effectively deployed the investment resources of the IFC and FIAS. In addition, the Bank and the IMF developed a robust, cooperative relationship.

Relevance and efficacy in other sectors has been uneven, despite good project-specific outcomes. Infrastructure, the quality of education, and bureaucratic quality have not kept up with the needs of a rapidly recovering economy in an integrated global marketplace. Bank assistance did not focus on assuring access by the poor to educational services until recently, and was limited in health and family planning. In the power sector, it was only partially helpful in coping with the crisis of 1990–92 and resolving the institutional and financial weaknesses of the public generation and transmission utility. The performance of the agriculture sec-

FIGURE 2.2: ONGOING PROJECTS: SUPERVISION RATINGS (AS OF OCTOBER 17, 1998)

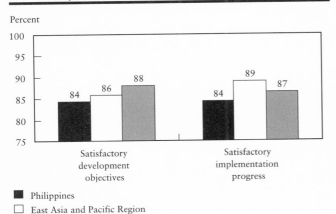

Percent

- Philippines
- East Asia and Pacific Region
- Bankwide

tor and the welfare of the poor remain negatively affected by high protective barriers on food products. Bank assistance fell short in supporting the government's agrarian reform until very recently. Thus, assistance over the years 1986–97 ranged from relevant and marginally satisfactory in some sectors (water and sanitation and transport) to poorly relevant or unsatisfactory in others (health, education, agriculture, and energy).[4] These sub-par ratings are attributed to various shortcomings of the institutional and policy environment, but also to the timing, design, or implementation of the Bank's lending and nonlending interventions.

Project-Specific Efficacy, Sustainability, and Institutional Development. The Bank's lending has improved considerably compared with its pre-1986 performance; it is now almost at par with EAP regional standards. About 92 percent of approved and completed projects (by value) received a satisfactory (or better) outcome rating, which is substantially higher than performance Bankwide (78 percent) and in the South Asia Region (72 percent), and only slightly lower than the performance of the EAP region (94 percent). The Philippines' ranking for likely sustainability is equally high, at 81 percent; its ratings for the institutional development impact of projects were higher (60 percent) than the EAP standard (52 percent).

All five adjustment operations approved since FY86 have earned satisfactory outcomes and likely sustainability ratings (a 100 percent success rate), and four had a substantial institutional development impact (the *Debt Management Program Loan* had a negligible institutional development (ID) impact because of the nature of the operation). For investment projects, the percentages of satisfactory outcomes, likely sustainability, and substantial institutional development for investment projects have also risen substantially since 1985, to 87 percent, 68 percent, and 43 percent respectively. Among the completed investment projects approved in the 1990s, unsatisfactory outcomes were recorded in energy, education, and microfinance operations.

Recent Project Portfolio. The Philippines had a healthy project portfolio through 1997. It was (and remains to date) the third-largest in the EAP Region, after China and Indonesia, both in total commitments ($2,212 million) and in the number of projects (23). Its performance was in line with EAP averages, which were better than those of any other region. Among the projects under implementation as of October 1997, 93 percent (by value) received a satisfactory rating for development objectives and 91 percent for implementa-

tion progress. These figures compared well with 93 and 90 percent, respectively, for the East Asia and Pacific Region.

More recent portfolio performance indicators (as of February 2, 1998) indicated a slight weakening of the Philippines' relative performance: 16 percent of commitments were at risk, compared with 13 percent for the region and 22 percent Bankwide, according to the Bank's Quality Assurance Group (QAG). Two projects—the *Highway Management* project and the *Urban Health and Nutrition* project—carried an unsatisfactory supervision rating for both development objectives and implementation progress. Two other projects—the *Manila 2nd Sewerage* project and the *Rural Electrification* project—were experiencing serious implementation delays. The most common reasons for poor performance were project management and procurement problems. Finally, the realism of supervision ratings among task managers had improved greatly, yielding small disconnect ratios between supervision and completion ratings.[5]

Efficiency. The overall cost of Bank assistance is within comparators' ranges. Other efficiency indicators appear within reasonable bounds. Both the total administrative budget and ESW resources declined appropriately, in parallel with the decline in lending commitments and the improvements in the country's economic and social performance.

The average cost of an ESW product over the ten-year period FY88–97 has been lower than in the EAP region, but significantly higher than in most other comparators except Indonesia. Although the average cost of lending per project is lower than the regional average and other comparators, the cost grew by 27 percent in staffweeks and 33 percent in direct dollar costs from FY85 to FY97. A large part of this increase can be attributed to the increase in dropped projects. This reflects important shifting government attitudes—first welcoming the Bank's intellectual and planning contributions, but then resorting to cheaper sources of financing among the donors. By FY97 the lending portfolio under supervision had shrunk by 44 percent since FY85 (with 50 projects) to 28 active projects. However, the cost of supervision increased, in line with the general trend in EAP and the Bank, reflecting the growing importance attached to portfolio management from FY94 onward. Projects in the Philippines had only a slightly higher cost of supervision, on average, than did EAP projects overall, but costs were significantly higher than in Malaysia and Thailand. The highest average cost of lending completion per project was in human resource development (more than 140 staffweeks), and the least in multisector lending (around 40 staffweeks). The completion costs in agriculture and public sector management were also among the highest.

Good Aid Coordination

The Bank has been active in coordinating and building consensus among donors and in the government through regular dialogues at both formal levels, by chairing Consultative Group (CG) meetings, and informal levels, and by arranging Manila-based working group meetings with other donors. The Bank supported the government's efforts to improve its own capacity and to assume an increasingly assertive position in aid coordination. Regular policy dialogue and the CG process helped the government to address the concerns of donors and to prioritize aid and budgetary allocations. Bank ESW and lending operations helped the government provide the donor community with clear policy frameworks to build and coordinate their own strategies. And Bank project preparation facilities helped the government prepare well-designed projects, and then tap the cheapest available financing sources. The government has increasingly assumed responsibility for program-level coordination and preparation for donor meetings.

The Bank has done a good job in helping to coordinate external assistance. It has recently pioneered efforts to add project copreparation activities to its cofinancing arrangements. Cofinancing has been effectively used. The government has been able to obtain additional concessional resources that individual donors would have found difficult to channel through their own project pipelines. And donors have been able to commit and disburse their available aid funds much more quickly, without compromising project quality.

The high priority placed on aid coordination by the Bank is evident in the high percentage of staffyears and budget spent on related activities against the total. Both in cost and time, the Philippines exceeds both the EAP average and the Bankwide average by a large degree all through this period: this is largely explained by the high frequency of CG and other donors' meetings. The Bank has used these resources well, consolidating its leadership in shaping the structural reforms and the public investment program. Overall, the Bank's emphasis on donor coordination was highly relevant and effective, because it fostered essential harmony among the major donors in the policy arena, without which the govern-

ment's reforms may have been delayed.

CG meetings have also provided an open forum for coordinating policy advice and different donor activities in the Philippines, monitoring progress in policy reforms and program/project implementation, providing opportunities and a clear agenda for many informal meetings around different topics, creating an opening for the government to take more leadership in aid coordination, and providing an opportunity for broader constituencies to air their views.

The Bank and NGO Partnership: A Maturing Relationship

The presence of a strong and diverse NGO community, a supportive government, and the knowledge and experience of donor agencies has created a favorable environment for stakeholder participation. The Bank has effectively promoted NGO participation at different levels of Bank operations, especially since the early 1990s. The increased openness of the Bank, particularly of the resident mission, over the past few years has been well received.

Project work done in the Philippines in the last three to five years has focused increasingly on ethnic minorities among the poor, and on participatory strategies with active community involvement. This is reflected in some of the targeting for the social sector projects and in natural resource management. For example, the *Conservation of Priority Protected Areas Project,* which covers a combination of protection of biodiversity, natural resource management, and community-based resource management, involves NGOs directly and focuses on the legalization of ancestral domainal lands of indigenous peoples.

Yet many NGOs remain skeptical about the Bank's conversion to participation. Some of their skepticism is merely a practical matter. For instance, although NGOs tend to see the Bank's consulting and procurement requirements as a sign of mistrust or imposition, this perception usually fades as they become more familiar with the operational environment of the Bank. But some of their skepticism stems from their resentment at being treated as less than full "partners." A few NGOs believe that their interest in policy formulation is deliberately played down by both the government and the Bank in favor of the "contractors" or the consultancy role. Some interpersonal mistrust is the result of occasional arrogance by Bank headquarters staff.

The Bank has generally been responsive to the needs of NGOs involved in projects. It has also learned lessons that it has integrated effectively into new project designs in irrigation, rural finance, health, and education. But it appears to be more interested in capacity-using than capacity-building, unlike other donors. The Bank does not track the status or number of NGO participants in Bank-funded projects after the completion of their involvement. And local representatives of donors working in NGO capacity-building activities have noted that the Bank does not risk working with NGOs in the formative stage, but takes the less risky route of selecting those with records of working well with other donors.

Unfulfilled Development Lending Potential

The Bank was not nimble at the outset of the Aquino administration, although it did release the undisbursed portion of its earlier *Agriculture Sector/Inputs Loan* to jump-start agricultural production. Reflecting the lagged effect of the previous slow-down in commitments, loan disbursements in 1986 bottomed-out at US$168 million and remained below US$300 million in 1987 and 1988. Bank staff believed that ensuring a positive net flow of resources from the Bank was not just desirable, but necessary to support continued growth and developing policy dialogue with government. And although senior management had autho-

rized about US$500 million in annual lending to the Aquino administration, in the four-year period FY86–89, the Bank fell 25 percent short of its lending plans. Lack of budgetary resources to process an adequate pipeline of projects on the part of the Bank was the main reason for the shortfall.

Lending commitments increased sharply to almost US$1,877 billion in FY90–91, as the Bank stepped-up its quick-disbursing balance of payments support and advanced several operations in the pipeline. These were, however, scaled back again, to between US$430 million and US$628 million in the next three years (FY92–94). This time, the reason was attributed to poor absorptive capacity by borrowing agencies, manifested by implementation problems in ongoing projects and delays in the preparation of new projects. During these years the Bank could have shifted back to adjustment lending to nurture policy reform. The policy debates within the country during the second half of the 1980s became much more contentious because of the negative resource transfer to the donor community. The pace of implementation of reforms might have been faster with more vigorous Bank involvement and less stringency.

Borrowing by the government from the Bank since 1994 has been consistently lower than the amounts the Bank was willing to make available, and less than what was appropriate to support the investment needs of a fast-recovering economy. During the most recent three-year period, FY95–97, commitments have averaged US$252 million a year. A decision in 1993 on the part of the government to limit further public borrowing from abroad (and, in consequence, from the Bank) appears to be the main reason for these low lending levels. The Bank had obtained Board endorsement for an annual lending program of around US$500 million.

The total net resource flow out of the country and to the Bank was US$2.7 billion during the period 1986–97, and was projected (December 1997) at US$536 million for 1998, and to rise in subsequent years. Such a large net negative resource flow at this early stage of the Philippines' development raises questions about the wisdom of phasing-out adjustment lending in the mid-1990s, with an agenda of structural reform still incomplete.[6]

Toward a New Country Assistance Strategy: Moving to a Higher Plane

Just as the Philippines has emerged stronger from the economic and social disarray that prevailed before 1986, it is likely to surmount the challenge posed by the current regional crisis. The resilience of the country and its people—tested repeatedly by domestic, natural, and global exigencies—augurs well for deeper and more rapid economic and social advancement in the wake of the Asian crisis. Its fallout provides an opportunity for policy and institutional reforms to fuel the economy's renewed competitiveness. The Philippines has the key factors to

move up the developmental ladder—political stability; broad consensus; government commitment; support from the donor community; an educated, skilled, hard-working, and English-speaking population; and now a 12-year record of good economic management. These positive conditions must now be mobilized to help the country gather momentum and make the leap needed to join the newly industrialized countries.

To help the economy reach its growth potential, fortify its capacity to withstand domestic and global exigencies, and reduce poverty, the Bank should focus its assistance on helping the government pursue and deepen its unfinished reform agenda. While expanding its liberalized environment—a valuable distinction from its neighbors—the country will need to apply the lessons of the East Asian miracle, as well as of those painfully drawn from the most recent East Asian crisis. Investment

levels must be increased and sustained with less volatile sources of financing. The country must shift the composition of foreign savings by tapping external sources of long-term funds to reduce the economy's dependence on future short-term capital flows. Poverty must be targeted directly, through broad-based programs beyond the trickle-down benefits from accelerated growth. Remaining policy and institutional constraints in the social sectors, in agriculture, in natural resource management, and in infrastructure must be eased or removed. Implementation capacity must be improved.

A new compact is needed among the government, the NGOs, the Bank, and the donor community to mobilize and use external assistance effectively. It should support a strong medium-term development program, backed by long-term sources of foreign savings and minimal competition among donors. Such an effort could

help the Philippines race ahead in social and economic progress during the next administration. The Bank should increase the selectivity of its nonlending assistance to improve the depth of its analysis and to increase participation. Lending assistance should be selective, in coordination with other donors, but also greater to support the unfinished reform agenda and the additional investment needs through a diversified set of instruments—quick-disbursing operations, financial intermediary loans, sector investment loans, guarantees, and new adaptable lending instruments. An expansion of budgetary resources allocated to the Philippines will be required to support such enlarged assistance.

Strengthening Macroeconomic Policy and Public Sector Management

In the very short term, the Bank should stand ready to offer, depending on the severity of the capital outflow and on the need for fair burden-sharing, emergency lending assistance to help ease the current liquidity shortage manifested in very high real interest rates. This could well take the form of an economic recovery loan, conditioned on the country entering a precautionary stand-by arrangement with the IMF, actions already taken, and the government's commitment to a comprehensive medium-term reform program. If used to increase the depleted official reserves, instead of for additional expenditures, the loan would directly reduce government refinancing requirements in the domestic capital market. This would lower market interest rates, reducing the severity of the economic slowdown for 1998. However, the Bank should move quickly beyond such emergency assistance to intensify support—beginning this year—for the reforms necessary to correct the macroeconomic weaknesses that have constrained high growth and left the economy vulnerable to downturns.

In the *financial sector,* Bank assistance should aim at strengthening the banking sector and the capital market so as to increase private sector savings, channel domestic and foreign savings more efficiently into investment, and minimize the impacts of future financial crises, domestic or global. A combination of action-oriented technical assistance and adjustment lending would be appropriate. The Bank could extend an adjustment loan with a technical assistance component to address the weaknesses remaining in the legal, regulatory, and supervisory regimes and in failure resolution for financial institutions. This loan could also support the correction of the distorted incentives that favor dollar over peso intermediation by the banking system, as well as other measures to manage future short-term capital flows. A technical assistance loan for housing finance reform, currently under preparation, might be expanded. Technical assistance by the Bank and IFC advisory services is also required to draw up an action plan for deepening the undeveloped bond market and for pension reform. With the country's demographics posing only a very distant threat to fiscal discipline, pension reform may not appear an urgent priority. However, it is one of the few instruments available to boost private savings. A capital market adjustment loan can then support the implementation of the agreed reforms.

In *public expenditure management*, a combination of regular public expenditure reviews, jointly conducted with the government, and adjustment lending is recommended to help restructure expenditures in favor of higher public investment and maintenance expenditures (in infrastructures and the social services) and to implement civil service reform. This operation could also support the introduction of equalization considerations in allocations across regions—and all units of local governments—and of incentives to strengthen the raising of local revenues. Other institutional measures to improve the efficiency of the bureaucracy (such as the recently adopted Anti-Corruption Initiative) and of public expenditure management (such as multiyear budgeting and rolling public investment programs) could also be supported by a combination of grants and technical assistance. For sectors with appropriate policies and institutions already in place, regular public expenditure reviews should open the door to sectoral investment and adaptable program loans with low conditionalities. The Bank should embark on an in-depth study of the judicial system and its options for reform in support of the country's economic development efforts and for serving the poor and vulnerable, followed by lending support to comprehensive judicial reform in the medium term.

Considering the initial conditions, much progress has already been achieved in openness, especially through *trade liberalization*, except for agricultural products. The recent depreciation of the peso offers the opportunity to go further in reducing import tariffs, especially on food products. In addition to boosting productivity as comparative advantage is allowed to operate, poor consumers (now heavily taxed by protection on food) would benefit from such liberalization. The Bank could support such a move with adjustment lending to help the government initiate the reform and provide a safety net for the poor and disadvantaged and compensatory measures for the displaced.

Supporting Private Sector Development and Basic Infrastructure

In addition to supporting reforms to improve the efficiency of the bureaucracies, the Bank Group should do more to help the private sector contribute to the solution of the problem of inadequate infrastructure. The *Private Sector Infrastructure Initiative* has already laid out the required elements to support a strategy of expanding private sector participation, but technical assistance is needed to complete the regulatory framework (for example, in the guidelines regarding government guarantees and the treatment of unsolicited proposals) governing private participation. A renewed Bank Group strategy is needed to lay out clearly the contributions of the Bank, IFC, and Multilateral Investment Guarantee Agency (MIGA) in support of private sector development, along the lines suggested in the 1994 *Private Sector Assessment* report. This is particularly important in light of the slow progress in expanding private activities in key sectors—particularly energy transmission, road and maritime transport, and water and sanitation beyond Manila.

In the right macroeconomic and institutional environment, which is expected to remain in force in the Philippines, the Bank can reinforce progress by supplementing the supply of private (mostly short- and medium-term) credit with long-term funds. Thus, the Bank should re-insert *financial intermediary loans*, including to SMEs, in its instrument menu. These loans can also support and extend financial sector reforms. With regard to microcredit, possibly the most direct and beneficial intervention for poverty alleviation in the medium term, the Bank should draw on experience, design an attractively simple vehicle, and offer funds for onlending to microenterprises. Here, the Bank could replicate other successful models with minimal study and processing costs, while studying and piloting innovations and improvements separately. To avoid limited use of technical assistance, a demand-driven and private-sector-oriented approach could be adopted in the design of technical assistance components.

In *power*, NPC urgently needs financial assistance before privatization. The Bank can help by linking future lending in the sector to congressional passage of legislation to allow NPC's privatization and to complete the regulatory framework for private participation. In light of the poor quality-at-entry ratings, the Bank should intensify supervision of the entire portfolio in the power sector. The Bank Group's goal for the short term should be to privatize virtually every dimension of the power sector and to put it on a sound commercial footing under a depoliticized regulatory framework. Once these conditions are in place, the IFC could do more to meet the sector's investment needs, and the Bank could shift its resources to support other infrastructure areas that are less financially attractive to private investors (and where the need for public investment remains substantial). In the meantime, intensified supervision (and possibly restructuring of some parts of the portfolio) will be needed to mitigate poor quality at entry.

For *water supply and sanitation,* the Bank Group should intensify its assistance to develop a sound regulatory framework and to quickly accomplish privatization outside Manila to demonstrate the process and present a model. This could go beyond current technical assistance proposals and policy notes, and include Bank guarantees and IFC advisory services and financial resources. A new Bank strategy should incorporate the findings of ADB's ongoing sector work and of the Bank study on institutional reforms of government-owned and controlled corporations (which includes the Local Water Utilities Administration, LWUA), and explicitly address the issue of future support for LWUA. The World Bank, the ADB, and the government should decide a joint donor policy for LWUA.

The Bank remains a large lender in this sector. Only a limited number of local government units and water districts may be suited for private sector participation (these being the larger systems, which hold promise for financial viability and progressive administration), but most will require a public sector approach for the next 5–7 years. As the same principle applies to other infrastructure sectors, and given the Bank success with graduating the beneficiaries of past loans for *Municipal Development* to the capital market, the Bank could continue, and indeed scale-up, its lending to include all noncreditworthy local government units. Such lending could include an expansion of the capacity-building compo-

nent (such as training provided by the Local Government Academy). A participatory strategy is urgently needed to assist local governments to cope with one of the fastest urbanization rates in the world and its infrastructure, social, and environmental implications.

Assistance to the *transport sector* falls in the same category. The Bank should continue to be active in transport, given the sector's important strategic place, the existing institutional weaknesses of the sector, the need for public investment, and the Bank's considerable experience in transport. But the Bank should adopt a participatory approach to the preparation of a detailed policy reform discussion paper and subsequent assistance strategy paper, including explicit discussion of phasing of individual reforms and an assessment of the losses and modalities for compensating the losers. Its sector work should focus—and Bank sector lending should be contingent—on the government addressing the five key remaining areas for reform: (i) privatizing road maintenance activities; (ii) establishing a Road Fund, a National Road Authority, and other related changes; (iii) introducing autonomy and increased private sector involvement in the port system and in the maritime sector in general; (iv) strengthening managerial and staff capacity in the transport sector, including the context of devolution to the provinces; and (v) encouraging competition.

Boosting Rural Development and Poverty Reduction

In the past few years, the Bank has made a determined effort to address more directly the situation of the rural poor. Recently approved projects in water resource management and agrarian community development are evidence of the Bank's renewed determination to adopt a more forceful strategy to reduce rural poverty. The recent Bank study, *Promoting Equitable Rural Growth* (1997), outlines a new comprehensive strategy for rural development, which is well timed to inform the planned participatory process to arrive at a new sector development strategy endorsed by the government, and subsequently to an agreed Bank assistance strategy.

Through synergy with a trade adjustment loan and associated sector lending, the Bank should support import tariff reductions for corn and other cereals, the removal of the rice monopoly and promotion of rice exports, and increased private sector participation in production, marketing, and distribution of agricultural products and inputs. The Bank should provide technical assistance (or undertake a joint study of public expenditures with the government and other major donors) to develop shared priorities for domestic and external resources expended in the sector. Areas that require more attention and resources in both the government's expenditure program and in the Bank's own lending and nonlending assistance are rural infrastructure and associated O&M, post-harvest facilities, and research and extension services.

Special efforts should be made to target assistance to the poor and to the regions where the poor live, and to involve the NGOs, local community organizations, and the beneficiaries in the review of ongoing projects and in the formulation and design of new ones (not only in their implementation). Two recently approved projects (the *Water Resources Development* project and the *Agrarian Reform Community Development* project) were designed in this direction. The Bank should expand its support for land reform, which is crucial for a more equitable distribution of assets. Beyond technical assistance to its beneficiaries, temporary budgetary support to help the government quickly complete its final phase of land reform will help reestablish certainty for the remaining landowners and revitalize private investment in the sector.

Finally, in *environmental protection and natural resources management*, the government lacks sufficient domestic resources (both human and local counterpart funding) to manage the recent surge in external funding assistance and to devise efficient ways to transfer some of these externally funded projects to the local governments. The Bank could provide technical assistance to help strengthen the institutional capacities of the relevant agencies in investment planning, project design and implementation, and to promote community-based approaches to protect the environment and improve the management of natural resources.

Revisiting Human Development

Given the Bank's limited and risky portfolio of ongoing projects in such critical sectors for poverty alleviation as health, population planning, and education, the Bank ought to give intense and immediate attention to supervision for all the ongoing projects and, failing a quick turnaround, to the restructuring of the *Urban Health and Nutrition* project. The government's reluctance to borrow externally (especially from the Bank) in these sectors has led to a series of projects that have been dropped after considerable energy had been spent in their preparation. Given the expected continuing availability of softer money within the donor community, the

Bank could consider dropping new lending initiatives in these sectors and allowing government and other donor resources to fill the void.

However, the Bank can and should continue to analyze policy and institutional constraints in all areas of health, family planning, education, and social protection and advise the government on future reforms and effective interventions. Supervision of the existing portfolio ought to be expanded from narrow project-related concerns to adequate monitoring and analysis of sector developments. Other donors' knowledge and sector work should be effectively absorbed. Future public expenditure reviews can then integrate, supplement, and analyze this information. It would be useful for the Bank to pull together the experiences in developing countries regarding the social returns to government investments in providing family planning, primary health care services, and improved quality of primary education in poor areas to make the argument for higher investment (and higher external long-term borrowing) for these purposes.

With respect to gender, it would require little effort to consult and better communicate with the agencies of government and women's groups on Bank gender studies and project-related activities. To this end, a modest extension to explore gender discrimination in the study of the Philippine labor market contained in the most recent economic report is recommended.

Should the Bank wish to remain an active lender in these sectors, it might look for an opportunity to lend for family planning, primary health care, and disease control with sector-type operations financing or cofinancing a time-slice of an agreed expenditure program. In education, the Bank should seek lending opportunities in primary education and limit its involvement with vocational and tertiary education to an advisory capacity.[1]

Mobilizing Partnerships

The Bank's ability to successfully deliver this refocused program of assistance would be enhanced by deepening its relationships with NGOs and civil society and enhancing their participation in the preparation of Bank strategy, ESW, and projects. The Bank should disseminate its policy views, strategy, and ESW outside government (albeit with its consent) to influence debate in civil society and parliament. While doing so, it should respect and support the strategies and priorities finally adopted by the country through its own consultative and democratic process.

The Bank should help the Philippines maximize long-term sources for required foreign savings through its own lending, continued aid coordination, and enhanced aid mobilization. It should also work to achieve better results on the ground at the sectoral level. Regular public expenditure reviews would be very valuable to donors in this respect. But the Bank should establish a new compact among the government, the Bank, and the donors. Although aid coordination by the Bank was praised by donors and government alike, there is much friendly (but wasteful) competition, especially in lending to the social sectors, and little reciprocal concern about other donors' results.

A more promising approach than each agency's proceeding with bilateral strategy discussions (or the project-specific multidonor copreparation/cofinancing route) would be a joint strategy and a clearer delineation of responsibilities, especially at the lending level, among donors. The process of preparing a joint CAS for all the major donors would help the government to enlarge its aid coordination efforts and leverage external assistance for maximum impact on the ground. The Bank has already piloted such an approach with its external assistance to Mindanao during the past two years. It is now time to scale-up such good partnership experience, building on the successes of the past. The process could begin with a broad agreement on a document akin to a Policy Framework Paper and matrix of medium-term reforms and sectoral development strategies, and could end with a matrix of each donor's proposed contribution. A truly participatory CAS covering all external assistance should be the Bank's goal by 1999.[2]

ENDNOTES

Chapter 1

1. In addition to their association with the failed Marcos regime, the net negative transfer of resources by the World Bank was another strong source of antipathy for the International Financial Institutions in the late 1980s.

Chapter 2

1. The Region disagrees with the conclusion that the Bank's assistance has been ineffective and unsatisfactory. The results have been mixed, according to the Region, partly because of the nature of the interventions (some well-intentioned projects were poorly designed), but mostly because of the vulnerability of the operations to the depth of the crisis in the 1980s.

2. The Region believes such a statement does not do justice to the efforts of the Bank's sectoral specialists. It reports that, while there were concerns in the energy team that the terms of the first BOT project were skewed too much in favor of Hopewell, and there was a danger that the government would end up paying for power it could not use, this was not a view shared by all. Through their contacts with investment bankers and BOT proponents, staff had helped create a more favorable climate for their involvement; the Bank had organized a roundtable on BOT opportunities (in power and other sectors), it had generally been supportive of the government's efforts, and most of its policy dialogue, including that on pricing, was crucial for setting the right foundations for the BOT operations.

3. The Bank objects to such characterization, as much of the analysis and discussion of the poverty report took place before the summit.

4. The Region disagrees with such characterization of Bank assistance in the health, education, agriculture, and energy sectors.

5. The performance of the most current portfolio (24 projects, $2.2 billion, as of October 1998), however, has deteriorated over the past year in both absolute and relative terms, mainly because of the effects of the financial crisis. Only 84 percent of projects under supervision are rated satisfactory, down from 93 percent. Three projects now carry an unsatisfactory rating for both development objectives and implementation progress (the *Transmission Grid Reinforcement* project, the *Urban Health and Nutrition* project, and the *Women's Health and Safety* project). A fourth project is deemed potentially at risk by QAG (the *Second Subic Bay* project). The country's portfolio performance, which continues to trail that of the region (86 percent), has recently fallen below the Bankwide average (88 percent).

6. In their comments to this report, BSP stressed that the net negative transfers during 1986–96 took place when the productivity of capital was high, while net positive transfers from the Bank took place during 1975–84, when the productivity of capital was comparatively low. BSP expressed want of a single, quantifiable estimate of the value of World Bank assistance to the country, one that would weigh appropriately the negative impact of the Bank's direct financial contribution to growth with its (presumably positive) indirect contributions to policy and institutional reforms, overall donors' aid levels, and international confidence.

Chapter 3

1. The Region disagrees with OED's recommendations to leave lending to others in the social sectors, as it believes that there is a lending role for the Bank, including in the reform of the vocational and higher education sectors, if the government were to take some difficult decisions.

2. The Region notes that discussions with the major donors in the context of the upcoming CAS preparation are planned, but that a joint CAS does not appear feasible, given other donors' constraints and the substantial additional costs involved—especially in light of the already relatively high spending on aid coordination noted in the report.

BIBLIOGRAPHY

Ahuja, V., and others. *Everyone's Miracle? Revisiting Poverty and Inequity in East Asia.* Washington, DC: World Bank, 1997.

Aiyer, Sri-Ram. *Anatomy of Mexico's Banking System Following the Peso Crisis.* Report No. 45 (Revised), Regional Studies Program, Latin America and the Caribbean Technical Department, Washington, DC: World Bank, December 1996.

Alegre, A.G. (ed.). *Trends and Traditions, Challenges and Choices: A Strategic Study of Philippine NGOs.* Ateno de Manila University, Manila, 1996.

Asian Development Bank. *Emerging Asia: Changes and Challenges.* Manila, 1997.

Baird, Michael. *Note on the Lessons for the World Bank of the Mexican Crisis.* Office of the SVP, Development Economics, Washington, DC: World Bank, June 1996.

Balisacan, A.M. "Agricultural Growth, Landlessness, Off-farm Employment and Rural Poverty in the Philippines." *Economic Development and Cultural Change,* Vol. 41, No. 3, pp. 533–562, 1993.

—— "Agricultural Growth, Policy Regime, and Rural Poverty in the Philippines." Draft Provisional Paper, Agriculture and Environment Operation Division, East Asia and Pacific Region, Washington, DC: World Bank, 1996.

Bhattacharya, Amar, Stijn Clasessens, and Leonardo Hernandez. "Recent Financial Market Turbulence in Southeast Asia: A Note." Washington, DC: World Bank, October 1997 (mimeo).

Binswanger, H.P. *The Policy Response of Agriculture.* Supplement to the *World Policy Economic Review* and the *World Bank Research Observer.*

Birdsall, N., D. Ross, and R. Sabot. "Inequality and Growth Reconsidered: Lessons from East Asia." *The World Bank Economic Review,* Vol. 9, No. 3, pp. 477–508, 1995.

Bordo, M. *Financial Crises.* Elgar Press, 1992.

Broad, Robin. *Unequal Alliance, The World Bank, the International Monetary Fund, and the Philippines.* Berkeley: University of California Press, 1988.

Caprio, G., and Daniela Klingebiel. "Bank Insolvency: Bad Luck, Bad Policy or Bad Banking?" Annual Bank Conference on Development Economics, April 25–26, Washington, DC: World Bank, 1996.

Chisholm, R. "Upland Natural Resources Strategy Paper." Draft Divisional Paper, Agriculture and Environment Operation Division, East Asia and Pacific Region (EA1AE), Washington, DC: World Bank, 1996.

Claessens, Stijn, and Thomas Glaessner. *Are Financial Sector Weaknesses Undermining the East Asian Miracle?* Washington, DC: World Bank, September 1997.

Clarke, G. "Participation and Protest: Non Governmental Organizations and Philippine Politics." Ph.D. Thesis, SOAS/University of London, 1995.

Cruz, C.M.J., I. Zosa, and C.L. Goce. "Population Pressure and Migration: Implications for Uplands Development in the Philippines," *Journal of Philippines Development,* Vol. 15, 1988.

David, C.C. "Policy Paper." Draft Divisional Paper, AE1AE, Washington, DC: World Bank, 1996.

Department of Agriculture. *Medium-term Agriculture Development Plan 1993–98.* DA, Quezon City, 1994.

Fry, Maxwell. *Money, Interest, and Banking in Economic Development,* 2d ed. Baltimore, MD: The Johns Hopkins University Press, 1995.

Galbis, Vincent. *Financial Sector Reforms in Eight Countries: Issues and Results.* IMF Working Paper, WP/95/141, Washington, DC, December, 1995.

Giles, Martin. "Coping with Ups and Downs, A Survey of International Banking," *The Economist*, April 27, 1996.

Hentschel, J. "Does Participation Cost the World Bank More? Emerging Evidence." Unpublished, Internet, June 1994.

Honohan, Patrick. "Preventing Financial System Crises." Washington, DC: IMF, March 1996 (mimeo).

Hutchcroft, Paul D. "Selective Squander: The Politics of Preferential Credit Allocation in the Philippines." In *The Politics of Finance in Developing Countries,* Hutchcroft and others, eds., Ithaca, NY: Cornell University Press, 1993.

IMF. *World Economic Outlook.* Washington, DC, December 1997.

Kaminsky, G., and Carmen Reinhart. "The Twin Crises: The Causes of Banking and Balance-of-Payments Problems." Washington, DC: IMF, February 1996 (mimeo).

Khatkhate, D. "A Review of Banking Crises: Cases and Issues, by Sundararajan and Balino." *Economic and Political Weekly,* 1992.

—— "Heretical Notes on Financial Reforms." Washington, DC: World Bank, n.d. (mimeo).

Khatkhate, D., and I. Dalla. *Regulated Deregulation of the Financial System in Korea.* World Bank Working Paper #292, Washington, DC, 1995.

Lugg, D. *Medium-term Agricultural Development Program: A Technical Review.* EA1AE, Washington DC: World Bank, 1996.

Magdaraog, G. L.L. "A Case Study of an NGO-GO-WB Dynamics in a GEF-funded Philippine Integrated Protected Areas Project." NIPA, April 1996.

Mason, A. "Will Population Change Sustain the 'Asian Economic Miracle'?" *Asia Pacific Issues,* No. 33, October 1997.

—— "Population Change in East Asia's Miracle Economies: Is there a Connection?" Paper presented at the Policy Seminar on Asian Economic Development: Long Term Perspective, Tokyo, October 20–21, 1997.

Medella, E. "An Assessment of the Philippine Economy: Trade and Industrial Policy." Draft report submitted to PIDS for the Assessment of the Philippine Economy Project, October 1997.

Meltzer, Allan. *Sustaining Safety and Soundness: Supervision, Regulation, and Financial Reform.* Washington, DC: World Bank, December 1995.

Mishkin, Frederic. "Understanding Financial Crises: A Developing Country Perspective." Annual Bank Conference on Development Economics, April 25–26, Washington, DC: World Bank, 1996.

Montes, Manuel F. *Stabilization and Adjustment Policies and Programmes, Country Study 2, The Philippines.* World Institute for Development Economics Research of the United Nations University, 1987.

NEDA. *Medium Term Philippine Development Plan, 1993–1998.* Manila, 1994.

—— "1995 Philippine Economic Performance and Prospects for 1996." Manila, 1996 (mimeo).

Office of the President. *The Vision of Philippines 2000.* The Coordinating Council of the Philippine Assistance Program, Manila, 1993.

Presidential Commission to Fight Poverty. *A Strategy to Fight Poverty.* Manila, 1994.

Reyes, Romeo. *Official Development Assistance to the Philippines: A Study of Administrative Capacity and Performance.* University of the Philippines, 1985.

Reitbergen-McCracken, J. (ed.). *Participation in Practice: The Experience of the World Bank and other Stakeholders.* Washington, DC: World Bank, December 1996.

Rojas-Suarez, Liliana, and Steven Weisbrod. *Financial Fragility in Latin America: The 1980s and 1990s.* Occasional Paper #132, Washington, DC: IMF, October 1995.

Selvavinayagam, K. "Medium-term Agricultural Development Plan: A General Review." Draft Divisional Paper, EA1AE, Washington, DC: World Bank, 1996.

Sachs, J. "Do We Need an International Lender of Last Resort?" *Princeton Studies in International Finance,* Department of Economics, Princeton University, 1996.

Sheng, Andrew. *Bank Restructuring: Lessons from the 1980s.* Washington, DC: World Bank, 1996.

Sundararajan, V., and T. Balino. *Banking Crises: Cases and Issues.* Washington, DC: IMF, 1991

Tan, E. *Effects of the Five Percent Uniform Tariff.* PIDS Discussion Paper No. 97-17, September 1997.

The Asian Society. *A Chronology of Recent Events in the Philippines.* August 1984.

Walden, Bello, David Kinley, and Elaine Elinson. *Development Debacle: The World Bank in the Philippines.* San Francisco, CA: Institute for Food and Development Policy (jointly with the Philippine Solidarity Network), 1982.

Walton, Michael. "The Maturation of the East Asian Miracle," *Finance and Development,* September 1997.

World Bank. *Sector Operations Review: Agricultural and Rural Development Program.* Report No. 3796-PHI. Washington, DC: World Bank, 1982.

—— *Philippines: Agriculture-Issues in Pricing Policy.* Report No. 4845-PH. Washington, DC: World Bank, 1984a.

—— *Philippines: Country Economic Memorandum.* Washington, DC: World Bank, 1984b.

—— *Philippines: Country Program Paper.* Washington, DC: World Bank, 1985a.

—— *The Philippines Food Processing Sector.* Report No. 5583-PH. Washington, DC: World Bank, 1985b.

—— *Philippines: Agricultural Sector Memorandum.* Report No. 6250-PH. Vols. I and II. Washington, DC: World Bank, 1986a.

—— "Philippines: 1986 Country Implementation Review of the World Bank-financed Projects. Background Paper." Washington, DC: World Bank, 1986a.

—— *The Philippines Sugarlands Diversification Study.* Report No. 6042-PH. Washington, DC: World Bank, 1986b.

—— *Agricultural Sector Strategy Review.* Report No. 6819-PH. Vols. I and II. Washington, DC: World Bank, 1987a.

—— *Philippine Agriculture: Its Present Condition and Future Needs.* Report No. 6613-PH. Washington, DC: World Bank, 1987b.

—— "Philippines: FY89 Country Program and Budget Paper." Internal Document. Washington, DC: World Bank, 1988a.

—— *The Philippines: The Challenge of Poverty.* Report No. 7144-PH. Washington, DC: World Bank, 1988b.

—— *Philippines: Forestry, Fisheries, and Agricultural Resource Management Study (FARM Study).* Report No. 7386-PH. (This study was later renamed *Philippines—Environment and Natural Resource Management Study.* Report No. 1 89-16502.) Washington, DC: World Bank, 1989.

—— *Philippines: Country Strategy Paper.* Washington, DC: World Bank, 1990a.

—— *Poverty. World Development Report 1990.* Washington, DC: World Bank, 1990b.

—— *Trade, Exchange Rate and Agricultural Pricing Policies in the Philippines.* Report No. 8485-PH. Washington, DC: World Bank, 1990c.

—— *World Development Report 1992: Development and Environment.* Washington, DC: World Bank, 1992.

—— *Philippines: Irrigated Agriculture Sector Review.* Report No. 9848-PH. Vols. I and II. Washington, DC: World Bank, 1992b.

—— *An Opening for Sustained Growth.* Report No. 11061-PH. Washington, DC: World Bank, 1993a.

—— *Philippines: Country Strategy Paper.* Washington, DC: World Bank, 1993b.

—— *Public Expenditure Management for Sustained and Equitable Growth.* Report No. 14680-PH. Washington, DC: World Bank, 1995.

—— *Country Assistance Strategy.* Report No. 15362-PH. Washington, DC: World Bank, 1996a.

—— *Philippines: A Strategy to Fight Poverty.* Washington, DC: World Bank, 1996b.

—— *Implementation Completion Report (ICR): Mexico-FSRL (Loan 3911-ME).* LAC Region, Washington, DC: World Bank. June 1997 (draft).

—— *Philippines: Promoting Equitable Rural Growth.* Draft Report No. 15782-PH. Washington, DC: World Bank, 1997.

ANNEX A

TABLE A.1: THE PHILIPPINES AT A GLANCE

	PHILIPPINES	EAST ASIA	LOWER-MIDDLE-INCOME
Poverty and Social Indicators			
Population mid-1996 *(millions)*	71.9	1,726	1,125
GNP per capita 1996 *(US$)*	1,160	890	1,750
GNP 1996 *(US$ billions)*	83.3	1,542	1,967
Average annual growth, 1990–96			
Population *(percent)*	2.3	1.3	1.4
Labor force *(percent)*	2.7	1.3	1.8
Most recent estimate *(latest year available since 1989)*			
Poverty: headcount index *(percent of population)*	54	..	..
Urban population *(percent of total population)*	55	31	56
Life expectancy at birth *(years)*	66	68	67
Infant mortality *(per 1,000 live births)*	37	40	41
Child malnutrition *(percent of children under 5)*	30	..	..
Access to safe water *(percent of population)*	85	49	78
Illiteracy *(percent of population age 15+)*	5	17	..
Gross primary enrollment *(percent of school-age population)*	116	117	104
Male	..	120	105
Female	..	116	101

DEVELOPMENT DIAMOND*

— Philippines
— Lower-middle-income group

Key Economic Ratios and Long-term Trends	1975	1985	1995	1996
GDP *(US$ billions)*	15.0	30.7	74.2	83.8
Gross domestic investment/GDP	30.9	15.3	22.2	24.2
Exports of goods and services/GDP	21.0	24.0	36.4	42.0
Gross domestic savings/GDP	24.8	17.4	14.4	14.4
Gross national savings/GDP	26.6	15.9	18.3	19.0
Current account balance/GDP	-6.2	-0.1	-4.4	-4.5
Interest payments/GDP	0.8	3.1	2.6	2.1
Total debt/GDP	27.8	86.6	53.2	49.2
Total debt service/exports	14.4	32.0	16.8	14.2
Present value of debt/GDP	..	..	..	46.1
Present value of debt/exports	..	..	..	95.0

	1975–85	1986–96	1995	1996	1997–05
(average annual growth)					
GDP	3.0	3.1	4.8	5.7	5.5
GNP per capita	0.3	1.3	2.6	4.5	3.5
Exports of goods and services	7.6	8.8	12.0	20.3	10.5

ECONOMIC RATIOS*

— Philippines
— Lower-middle-income group

* The diamonds show four key indicators in the country (in bold) compared with its income-group average. If data are missing, the diamond will be incomplete.

Note: Data for 1996 are preliminary estimates.

(table continued on following page)

TABLE A.1: THE PHILIPPINES AT A GLANCE (CONTINUED)

GROWTH RATES OF OUTPUT AND INVESTMENT (%)

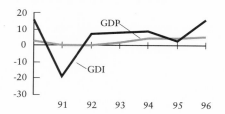

GROWTH RATES OF EXPORTS AND IMPORTS (%)

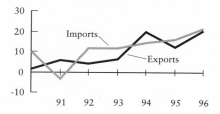

INFLATION (%)

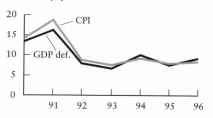

EXPORT AND IMPORT LEVELS (MILL. US$)

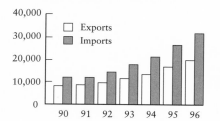

Structure of the Economy	1975	1985	1995	1996
(percent of GDP)				
Agriculture	30.3	24.6	21.6	21.4
Industry	34.6	35.1	32.1	31.7
Manufacturing	25.7	25.2	23.0	22.6
Services	35.0	40.4	46.3	46.9
Private consumption	64.5	75.0	74.2	73.9
General government consumption	10.7	7.6	11.4	11.7
Imports of goods and services	27.1	21.9	44.2	51.7

	1975–85	1986–96	1995	1996
(average annual growth)				
Agriculture	2.2	1.8	0.8	3.0
Industry	2.6	3.2	7.0	6.3
Manufacturing	1.8	3.1	6.8	5.6
Services	3.8	3.8	5.0	6.5
Private consumption	3.3	3.9	8.5	5.3
General government consumption	0.4	4.2	5.4	5.2
Gross domestic investment	-0.4	6.7	3.0	15.6
Imports of goods and services	3.9	12.0	16.0	21.1
Gross national product	2.7	3.8	5.0	6.9

Prices and Government Finance	1975	1985	1995	1996
Domestic prices *(percent change)*				
Consumer prices	6.8	23.1	8.1	8.4
Implicit GDP deflator	9.3	17.6	7.5	9.0
Government finance *(percent of GDP)*				
Current revenue	..	12.1	18.8	19.5
Current budget balance	..	2.4	3.4	3.1
Overall surplus/deficit	..	..	-1.4	-0.4

Trade	1975	1985	1995	1996
(US$ millions)				
Total exports (fob)	..	4,629	16,720	19,809
Coconut oil	..	347	826	571
Sugar	..	185	66	136
Total imports (cif)	..	5,111	26,391	31,885
Food	..	256	1,204	1,578
Fuel and energy	..	1,452	2,461	3,008
Capital goods	..	769	8,029	10,472
Export price index *(1987=100)*	..	81	124	124
Import price index *(1987=100)*	..	63	128	137
Terms of trade *(1987=100)*	..	127	97	90

Note: Data for 1996 are preliminary estimates.

TABLE A.1: THE PHILIPPINES AT A GLANCE (CONTINUED)

Balance of Payments	1975	1985	1995	1996
(US$ millions)				
Exports of goods and services	3,000	6,864	21,978	28,708
Imports of goods and services	4,116	5,961	33,314	42,254
Resource balance	-1,116	903	-11,336	-13,546
Net income	-126	-1,317	7,157	9,185
Net current transfers	318	379	882	589
Current account balance, before official capital transfers	-923	-35	-3,297	-3,772
Financing items (net)	912	867	3,928	7,879
Changes in net reserves	11	-832	-631	-4,107
Memo:				
Reserves including gold *(US$ millions)*	1,458	1,098	7,755	11,717
Conversion rate *(local/US$)*	7.2	18.6	25.7	26.2

CURRENT ACCOUNT BALANCE TO GDP RATIO (%)

External Debt and Resource Flows	1975	1985	1995	1996
(US$ millions)				
Total debt outstanding and disbursed	4,171	26,637	39,446	41,214
IBRD	238	2,421	5,002	4,666
IDA	17	84	183	193
Total debt service	457	2,534	5,337	5,778
IBRD	26	285	789	766
IDA	0	1	3	3
Composition of net resource flows				
Official grants	72	139	276	246
Official creditors	185	360	-626	-310
Private creditors	348	796	1,141	1,859
Foreign direct investment	98	12	1,478	1,408
Portfolio equity	0	0	1,961	1,333
World Bank program				
Commitments	114	104	168	528
Disbursements	94	276	402	457
Principal repayments	12	110	415	426
Net flows	82	166	-13	31
Interest payments	14	176	377	343
Net transfers	68	-10	-390	-312

COMPOSITION OF TOTAL DEBT, 1996 (MILL. US$)

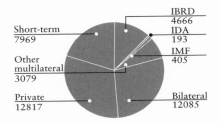

Note: Data for 1996 are preliminary estimates.

TABLE A.2: SUMMARY OF PROJECT INFORMATION: THE PHILIPPINES

TOTAL APPROVED PROJECTS[a]

	Number	Percent	Value ($m)	Percent
Adjustment loans	9	6	2,076.3	20
Nonadjustment loans	140	94	8,082.0	80
Total	**149**	**100**	**10,158.3**	**100**

OED OUTCOME RATINGS

	Number	Percent	Value ($m)	Percent
Satisfactory outcome				
Adjustment loans	6	75	1,350.0	73
Nonadjustment loans	79	76	3,610.0	80
Total	**85**	**76**	**4,960.0**	**78**
Unsatisfactory outcome				
Adjustment loans	2	25	502.0	27
Nonadjustment loans	25	24	924.5	20
Total	**27**	**24**	**1,426.7**	**22**
TOTAL RATED	**112**		**6,386.7**	

OED SUSTAINABILITY RATINGS

	Number	Percent	Value ($m)	Percent
Likely sustainability				
Adjustment loans	5	83	1,200.0	89
Nonadjustment loans	36	57	2,253.5	67
Total likely sustainability	**41**	**59**	**3,453.5**	**73**
Uncertain sustainability				
Adjustment loans	1	17	150.0	11
Nonadjustment loans	16	25	544.7	16
Total uncertain sustainability	**17**	**25**	**694.7**	**15**
Unlikely sustainability				
Adjustment loans	0	0	0.0	0
Nonadjustment loans	11	17	554.1	17
Total unlikely sustainability	**11**	**16**	**554.1**	**12**
TOTAL RATED	**69**	**100**	**4,702.3**	**100**

OED INSTITUTIONAL DEVELOPMENT RATINGS

	Number	Percent	Value ($m)	Percent
Substantial ID				
Adjustment loans	4	67	1,000.0	74
Nonadjustment loans	21	36	1,194.4	39
Total substantial ID	**25**	**38**	**2,194.4**	**49**
Moderate ID				
Adjustment loans	1	17	150.0	11
Nonadjustment loans	25	42	1,328.8	43
Total moderate ID	**26**	**40**	**1,478.8**	**33**
Negligible ID				
Adjustment loans	1	17	200.0	15
Nonadjustment loans	13	22	561.0	18
Total negligible ID	**14**	**22**	**761.0**	**17**
TOTAL RATED	**65**	**100**	**4,434.7**	**100**

TOTAL APPROVED PROJECTS, BY PERIOD (FY)

Period	Number	Percent	Value ($m)	Percent
1958–80	73	49	2,512.1	25
1981–85	26	17	1,925.8	19
1986–89	13	9	1,493.6	15
1990–98*	37	25	4,226.8	42
TOTAL	**149**	**100**	**10,158.3**	**100**

OED SATISFACTORY OUTCOME RATINGS BY PERIOD[b]

	Loans Rated	% Satisfact.	Value ($m)	% Satisfact.
1958–80				
Adjustment loans	6	75	1,350.0	73
Adjustment loans	0		0.0	
Nonadjustment loans	65	74	2,211.9	72
Period total	**65**	**74**	**2,211.9**	**72**
1981–85				
Adjustment loans	3	33	652.2	23
Nonadjustment loans	22	77	689.2	86
Period total	**25**	**72**	**1,341.4**	**55**
1986–89				
Adjustment loans	3	100	800.0	100
Nonadjustment loans	8	100	509.4	100
Period total	**11**	**100**	**1,309.4**	**100**
1990–97				
Adjustment loans	2	100	400.0	100
Nonadjustment loans	9	67	1,124.0	81
Period total	**11**	**73**	**1,524.0**	**86**
All: 1958–97				
Adjustment loans	8	75	1,852.2	73
Nonadjustment loans	104	76	4,534.5	80
TOTAL RATED	**112**	**76**	**6,386.7**	**78**

ARPP RATINGS OF ONGOING PROJECTS

	Number	Percent	Value ($m)	Percent
Development objectives				
Satisfactory	22	96	2,062.4	93
Unsatisfactory	1	4	150.0	7
TOTAL	**23**	**100**	**2,212.4**	**100**
Implementation progress				
Satisfactory	21	91	2,005.4	91
Unsatisfactory	2	9	207.0	9
TOTAL	**23**	**100**	**2,212.4**	**100**

DISCONNECT FOR PHILIPPINES

Number of projects	ARPP % Sat.	OED % Sat.	Net disc. at exit[c]
99	92	76	16%

Note: Includes projects evaluated through October 6, 1997.
a. Through December 1997.
b. Based on FY of Board approval.
c. Based on projects evaluated by OED through October 6, 1997. The disconnect is the difference between the share of projects rated satisfactory during the last supervision year and the share of projects rated satisfactory after completion. Thus it is an indication of the optimism in supervision ratings.
Source: OIS, FDB.

TABLE A.3: COMPLETED AND EVALUATED PROJECTS (THROUGH OCTOBER 6, 1997)

PROJECT NAME	OUT-COME[1]	SUST[2]	INST[3]	INVESTMENT/ADJUSTMENT	NET COMMIT. (US$M)	APPROVAL DATE	LATEST REPORT TYPE	LATEST REPORT NUMBER	LATEST REPORT DATE	EVALUATION YEAR	OED ID
Agriculture (38)											
Second rural credit	S			I	12.5	27-May-69	PAR	01277	18-Aug-76	1976	L0607
Upper Pampanga River irrigation	S			I	33.9	12-Aug-69	PAR	03063	30-Jun-80	1980	L0637
Rice processing and storage	S			I	14.3	26-Jan-71	PAR	04554	15-Jun-83	1983	L0720
Livestock development	S			I	7.5	04-May-72	PAR	02128	30-Jun-78	1978	L0823
Fisheries credit	S			I	11.6	15-May-73	PAR	04222	13-Dec-82	1982	L0891
Aurora – Penaranda irrigation	S			I	18.9	30-Apr-74	PAR	04555	16-Jun-83	1983	L0984
Third rural credit	S			I	22.0	11-Jun-74	PAR	02784	27-Dec-79	1979	L1010
Tarlac irrigation systems improvement	S			I	17.0	17-Dec-74	PAR	05969	12-Dec-85	1985	L1080
Rural development	S			I	25.0	08-Apr-75	PAR	05978	18-Dec-85	1985	L1102
Magat River multipurpose	S	Lik	Napl	I	42.0	22-Jul-75	PAR	07923	30-Jun-89	1989	L1154
Second livestock development	S			I	20.5	16-Mar-76	PAR	04753	21-Oct-83	1983	L1225
Chico River irrigation	U	Unc	Napl	I	50.0	23-Mar-76	PAR	07923	30-Jun-89	1989	L1227
Second grain processing	S			I	11.5	25-May-76	PCR	05448	06-Feb-85	1985	L1269
Second fisheries	S			I	12.0	25-May-76	PAR	04222	13-Dec-82	1982	L1270
Jalaur irrigation	S			I	14.9	01-Feb-77	PAR	05969	12-Dec-85	1985	L1367
Fourth rural credit	S			I	36.5	05-Apr-77	PCR	06016	31-Dec-85	1985	L1399
National irrigation systems improvement	U	Lik	Sub	I	38.2	03-May-77	PAR	10669	22-May-92	1990	L1414
Rural development II (land settlement)	U	Unc	Neg	I	13.0	17-May-77	PCR	10175	16-Dec-91	1991	L1421
Smallholder tree farming and forestry	U		Sub	I	4.2	22-Dec-77	PAR	07585	31-Dec-88	1988	L1506
Second national systems improvement	U	Lik	Sub	I	48.7	28-Feb-78	PAR	10669	22-May-92	1989	L1526
First rural infrastructure	S	Unc	Neg	I	21.5	11-Apr-78	PAR	07936	30-Jun-89	1989	C0790
Magat River multipurpose, stage two	S	Lik	Napl	I	149.6	11-May-78	PAR	07923	30-Jun-89	1989	L1567
National extension	U			I	20.0	07-Nov-78	PAR	07286	13-Jun-88	1988	L1626
Second Magat River multipurpose, stage two	S	Lik	Napl	I	26.1	12-Dec-78	PAR	07923	30-Jun-89	1989	L1639
Small farmer development land bank	U	Unc	Mod	I	15.7	21-Dec-78	PCR	10349	21-Feb-92	1992	L1646
Samar Island rural development	U	Unl	Mod	I	27.0	04-Dec-79	PCR	09208	21-Dec-90	1990	L1772
Medium-scale irrigation	U	Unl	Sub	I	33.0	13-Mar-80	PCR	11511	30-Dec-92	1992	L1809
Rainfed agricultural development (ILOILO)	S	Lik	Mod	I	5.3	20-Mar-80	PAR	07949	30-Jun-89	1989	L1815
Watershed management and erosion control	U	Unl	Mod	I	32.8	08-Jul-80	PAR	16408	27-Mar-97	1991	L1890
Third livestock and fisheries credit	S	Unc	Mod	I	23.5	15-Jul-80	PCR	07871	28-Jun-89	1989	L1894
Agricultural support services	U	Unc	Mod	I	19.9	14-Jul-81	PAR	15223	29-Dec-95	1992	L2040
National fisheries development	U	Unl	Neg	I	1.9	25-May-82	PCR	09891	16-Sep-91	1991	L2156
Communal irrigation development	S	Lik	Sub	I	38.1	08-Jun-82	PCR	11512	29-Dec-92	1992	L2173
Central Visayas regional development	S	Lik	Mod	I	22.1	06-Dec-83	PAR	16661	10-Jun-97	1993	L2360
Agricultural sector/inputs	S	Unc	Mod	A	150.0	04-Sep-84	PAR	10314	10-Feb-92	1990	L2469
Agricultural credit	S	Lik	Mod	I	100.0	06-Jun-85	PAR	10969	28-Jul-92	1991	L2570
Irrigation operations support	S	Lik	Sub	I	23.5	02-Jun-88	PCR	13826	29-Dec-94	1994	L2948
Rural finance	S	Lik	Mod	I	150.0	21-Jun-91	PCR	15233	31-Jan-96	1996	L3356

(table continued on following page)

TABLE A.3: COMPLETED AND EVALUATED PROJECTS (THROUGH OCTOBER 6, 1997) (CONTINUED)

PROJECT NAME	OUT-COME[1]	SUST[2]	INST[3]	INVESTMENT/ ADJUSTMENT	NET COMMIT. (US$M)	APPROVAL DATE	LATEST REPORT TYPE	LATEST REPORT NUMBER	LATEST REPORT DATE	EVALUATION YEAR	OED ID
Education (9)											
Agricultural education	S			I	5.9	13-Oct-64	PAR	00820	30-Jul-75	1975	L0393
Second education	S			I	12.7	12-Dec-72	PAR	04162	01-Nov-82	1982	C0349
Third education	S			I	24.7	16-Mar-76	PAR	06279	27-Jun-86	1986	L1224
Fourth education	S			I	24.9	01-Mar-77	PAR	06348	17-Jul-86	1986	L1374
Educational radio technical assistance	S			I	1.2	21-Mar-78	PCR	05004	23-Mar-84	1984	LS008
Fishery training	U	Unl	Neg	I	35.1	18-Dec-79	PAR	08788	25-Jun-90	1990	L1786
Elementary education sector loan	S	Lik	Sub	I	80.0	30-Jun-81	PAR	12632	29-Dec-93	1991	L2030
Vocational training	S	Lik	Sub	I	14.9	21-Sep-82	PAR	13062	17-May-94	1992	L2200
Second elementary education	U	Unl	Neg	I	175.0	03-Jul-90	EVM			1997	L3244
Electric Power and Other Energy (9)											
Fourth power	S			I	12.0	04-Apr-67	PAR	00980	16-Jan-76	1976	L0491
Fifth power	S			I	31.8	21-Mar-72	PCR	04388	16-Mar-83	1983	L0809
Sixth power	S			I	60.5	02-Jul-74	PCR	04847	22-Dec-83	1983	L1034
Seventh power	S	Lik	Mod	I	58.0	14-Jun-77	PAR	08574	20-Apr-90	1990	L1460
Rural electrification	S			I	60.0	04-Apr-78	PAR	05732	24-Jun-85	1985	L1547
Geothermal exploration	S	Lik	Sub	I	8.2	30-Sep-82	PAR	09667	21-Jun-91	1990	L2203
Bacon-Manito geothermal power	S	Lik	Sub	I	93.6	23-Jun-88	EVM			1996	L2969
Manila power distribution	S	Lik	Mod	I	59.8	08-Jun-89	EVM			1997	L3084
Energy Sector[4]	S	Lik	Sub	I	370.6	01-Feb-90	EVM			1997	L3163
Finance (11)											
Third development corporation	S			I	23.7	01-Jul-69	PAR	01576	29-Apr-77	1977	L0630
Industrial investment and smallholder tree-farmers	U			I	49.6	11-Jun-74	PAR	05744	28-Jun-85	1985	L0998
Fourth development corporation	S	Lik	Sub	I	29.8	05-Nov-74	PAR	08781	21-Jun-90	1983	L1052
Second industrial investment credit	U			I	75.0	16-Dec-75	PAR	05744	28-Jun-85	1985	L1190
Fifth development corporation	S	Unc	Sub	I	29.3	31-Jan-78	PAR	08781	21-Jun-90	1989	L1514
Investment systems organization	S			I	14.5	27-Apr-78	PCR	06006	27-Dec-85	1985	L1555
Third industrial investment credit	U	Unl	Neg	I	71.2	18-May-78	PAR	08781	21-Jun-90	1990	L1572
Industrial finance	S	Lik	Sub	I	44.6	07-May-81	PAR	08781	21-Jun-90	1990	L1984
Financial sector adjustment	S	Lik	Sub	A	300.0	04-May-89	PAR	15834	28-Jun-96	1995	L3049
Industrial investment credit	S	Lik	Mod	I	65.0	05-Oct-89	PCR	12127	30-Jun-93	1993	L3123
Cottage enterprise finance	U	Unl	Neg	I	1.5	26-Mar-91	PAR	15834	28-Jun-96	1995	L3312
Industry (6)											
Small and medium industries development	S			I	30.0	27-May-75	PAR	03969	16-Jun-82	1982	L1120
Second small and medium industries development	S	Lik	Sub	I	24.9	12-Jun-79	PAR	08781	21-Jun-90	1989	L1727
Textile sector restructuring	U	Unl	Mod	I	15.4	20-Apr-82	PCR	08107	06-Oct-89	1989	L2127
Third small and medium industries development	S	Lik	Mod	I	63.2	03-Jun-82	PAR	08781	21-Jun-90	1990	L2169

TABLE A.3: COMPLETED AND EVALUATED PROJECTS (THROUGH OCTOBER 6, 1997) (CONTINUED)

PROJECT NAME	OUT-COME[1]	SUST[2]	INST[3]	INVESTMENT/ ADJUSTMENT	NET COMMIT. (US$M)	APPROVAL DATE	LATEST REPORT TYPE	LATEST REPORT NUMBER	LATEST REPORT DATE	EVALUATION YEAR	OED ID
Fourth small and medium industrial development	S	Lik	Neg	I	60.0	25-Apr-89	PCR	14055	15-Mar-95	1995	L3038
Industrial restructuring	S	Lik	Sub	I	175.0	08-Jan-91	EVM			1996	L3287
Mining (1)											
Coal exploration	S	Unc	Sub	I	6.6	15-Jun-82	PAR	09667	21-Jun-91	1987	L2181
Multisector (6)											
Structural adjustment loan	U			A	200.0	16-Sep-80	PAR	05813	31-Jul-85	1985	L1903
Second structural adjustment loan	U			A	302.3	26-Apr-83	PAR	05813	31-Jul-85	1985	L2266
Economic recovery program	S	Lik	Sub	A	300.0	17-Mar-87	PAR	10866	30-Jun-92	1992	L2787
Debt management program	S	Lik	Neg	A	200.0	21-Dec-89	PAR	14811	30-Jun-95	1993	L3149
Earthquake reconstruction	S	Unc	Mod	I	109.3	09-Oct-90	EVM			1997	L3263
Economic integration	S	Lik	Sub	A	200.0	10-Dec-92	EVM			1996	L3539
Oil and Gas (2)											
Petroleum exploration promotion	S	Lik	Sub	I	7.8	30-Sep-82	PAR	09667	21-Jun-91	1990	L2201
Petroleum exploration promotion	S	Lik	Sub	I	7.3	30-Sep-82	PAR	09667	21-Jun-91	1990	L2202
Population, Health, and Nutrition (2)											
Population	U			I	23.3	02-Jul-74	PAR	05544	19-Mar-85	1985	L1035
Second population	U	Unc	Neg	I	32.2	05-Jun-79	PAR	09380	15-Feb-91	1991	C0923
Public Sector Management (2)											
Economic recovery technical assistance	NRAT	Unc	Neg	I	0.0	17-Mar-87	PAR	10866	30-Jun-92	1992	L2788
Program for government corporation	S	Lik	Sub	A	200.0	15-Jun-88	PAR	15614	13-May-96	1993	L2956
Telecommunications (1)											
Telecommunications technical assistance	S	Lik	Mod	I	4.0	19-Feb-85	PCR	09609	31-May-91	1991	L2495
Transportation (11)											
Highway	S			I	8.0	06-Apr-71	PAR	02449	02-Apr-79	1979	L0731
Second port	S			I	6.0	16-Oct-73	PAR	05698	07-Jun-85	1985	L0939
Second highway	S			I	68.0	04-Dec-73	PAR	04757	25-Oct-83	1983	L0950
Shipping	S			I	19.4	15-Oct-74	PAR	04910	31-Jan-84	1984	L1048
Third highway	S			I	95.0	23-Dec-76	PAR	07316	30-Jun-88	1988	L1353
Fourth highway	S	Lik	Mod	I	99.6	06-Mar-79	PCR	08053	07-Sep-89	1989	L1661
Third port	U			I	66.9	27-May-80	PCR	07570	31-Dec-88	1988	L1855
Rural roads improvement	S	Unc	Mod	I	50.2	29-May-80	PCR	09522	15-Apr-91	1991	L1860
Fifth highway	S	Lik	Neg	I	90.9	17-May-84	EVM	15503	08-Apr-96	1995	L2418
Second rural roads improvement	S	Unc	Mod	I	81.9	10-Jun-86	EVM			1996	L2716
Provincial ports	S	Lik	Neg	I	30.1	26-May-87	PCR	14712	26-Jun-95	1995	L2823

(table continued on following page)

TABLE A.3: COMPLETED AND EVALUATED PROJECTS (THROUGH OCTOBER 6, 1997) (CONTINUED)

PROJECT NAME	OUT-COME[1]	SUST[2]	INST[3]	INVESTMENT/ ADJUSTMENT	NET COMMIT. (US$M)	APPROVAL DATE	LATEST REPORT TYPE	LATEST REPORT NUMBER	LATEST REPORT DATE	EVALUATION YEAR	OED ID
Urban Development (8)											
Manila urban development	S			I	39.3	27-May-76	PAR	07092	19-Jan-88	1986	L1272
Second urban development	S			I	30.5	21-Dec-78	PAR	07092	19-Jan-88	1988	L1647
Third urban development	S	Lik	Mod	I	67.1	25-Mar-80	PCR	07897	30-Jun-89	1989	L1821
Urban engineering	S			I	7.3	08-Dec-81	PCR	07009	16-Nov-87	1987	L2067
Regional cities development	S	Unl	Mod	I	35.9	31-Mar-83	PAR	14780	30-Jun-95	1995	L2257
Municipal development	S	Lik	Sub	I	35.8	05-Jun-84	PAR	16800	27-Jun-97	1995	L2435
Housing sector	S	Unl	Mod	I	125.3	24-Jun-88	PCR	15810	25-Jun-96	1996	L2974
Second municipal development	S	Lik	Sub	I	40.0	14-Dec-89	PAR	16800	27-Jun-97	1997	L3146
Water Supply and Sanitation (7)											
Provincial cities water supply	S			I	21.8	03-May-77	PAR	06422	29-Sep-86	1986	L1415
Second Manila water supply	S	Unc	Mod	I	88.0	25-Jul-78	PCR	07153	04-Mar-88	1988	L1615
Second provincial cities water supply	U	Lik	Sub	I	25.0	29-May-79	PCR	08937	27-Jul-90	1990	C0920
Manila sewerage and sanitation	S	Unc	Neg	I	44.5	20-Mar-80	PAR	13204	24-Jun-94	1990	L1814
Rural water supply and sanitation	U			I	28.9	19-Oct-82	PCR	10225	17-Dec-91	1991	L2206
Metropolitan Manila water distribution	S	Lik	Mod	I	35.3	03-Apr-86	PCR	14293	11-Apr-95	1995	L2676
Angat water supply optimal	U	Unc	Mod	I	37.6	05-Oct-89	EVM			1997	L3124

1. Outcome ratings: S = satisfactory, U = unsatisfactory.
2. Sustainability ratings: Lik = likely, Unc = uncertain, Unl = unlikely, Nrat = not rated.
3. Institutional Development Impact ratings: Sub = substantial, Mod = modest, Neg = negligible, Napl = not applicable.
4. A recent but not yet finalized OED audit is proposing to downgrade all the project completion ratings.

TABLE A.4: ONGOING AND RECENTLY COMPLETED PROJECTS

PROJECT NAME	STATUS	LATEST DEVELOPMENT OBJECTIVES SUPERVISION RATING	LATEST IMPLEMENTATION PROGRESS SUPERVISION RATING	QUALITY ASSURANCE GROUP (QAG) RISK RATING (2/26/98)	OED QUALITY AT ENTRY RATING	INVESTMENT OR ADJUSTMENT OPERATION	BOARD APPROVAL DATE	EFFECTIVENESS DATE	CLOSING DATE
Agriculture (7)									
Coconut farms development	Active	S	S	Nonrisky	Satisfactory	I	5/24/90	11/14/90	6/30/98
Second communal irrigation	Active	S	S	Nonrisky	Unsatisfactory	I	10/4/90	1/11/91	12/31/98
Environment and natural resource management	Active	S	S	Nonrisky	Unsatisfactory	A	6/25/91	10/10/91	12/31/98
Second irrigation operational support	Active	S	S	Nonrisky	Satisfactory	I	5/20/93	10/15/93	6/30/99
Second rural finance	Active	S	S	Nonrisky	Satisfactory	I	9/14/95	4/23/96	6/30/02
Water resources development	Active	S	S	Nonrisky	Highly satisfactory	I	11/26/96	3/20/97	12/31/02
Agrarian reform communication	Active	S	S	Nonrisky	Satisfactory	I	11/26/96	4/8/97	12/31/03
Education (3)									
Engineering and science	Active	S	S	Nonrisky	Highly unsatisfactory	I	1/28/92	6/3/92	6/30/98
Second vocational training	Active	S	S	Nonrisky	Highly unsatisfactory	I	6/18/92	12/11/92	12/31/98
Third elementary education	Active	S	S	Nonrisky	Highly satisfactory	I	11/26/96	7/2/97	6/30/04
Electric Power and Energy (5)									
Rural electrification	Active	S	U	Actual	Unsatisfactory	I	2/25/92	10/22/92	4/30/98
Power transmission and rehabilitation	Completed	S	S	Nonrisky	Unsatisfactory	I	6/22/93	12/6/93	12/31/97
Leyte Cebu geothermal	Active	S	S	Nonrisky	Unsatisfactory	I	2/3/94	7/18/94	6/30/98
Leyte Luzon geothermal	Active	S	S	Nonrisky	Highly unsatisfactory	I	6/7/94	3/1/95	6/30/99
Trans Grid reinforcement	Active	S	S	Nonrisky	Unsatisfactory	I	4/4/96	11/12/96	12/31/00
Industry (1)									
Second Subic Bay	Active	n.a.	n.a.	Nonrisky	Satisfactory	I	11/26/96	10/15/97	12/31/00
Population, Health, and Nutrition (3)									
Health development	Completed	S	S	Actual	Satisfactory	I	6/22/89	1/10/90	12/31/97
Urban health and nutrition	Active	U	U	Nonrisky	Satisfactory	I	6/8/93	4/7/94	12/31/00
Womens' health and safety	Active	S	S	Nonrisky	Satisfactory	I	3/9/95	7/27/95	12/31/01
Public Sector Management (1)									
Tax computerization	Active	S	S	Nonrisky	Highly satisfactory	I	5/11/93	12/1/93	6/30/99
Telecommunications (1)									
Telephone system expansion	Completed	S	S	Nonrisky	Highly satisfactory	I	n.a.	n.a.	12/31/98
Transportation (2)									
Highway management	Active	U	U	Actual	Satisfactory	I	12/20/91	6/1/92	6/30/99
Subic Bay freeport	Active	HS	S	Nonrisky	Satisfactory	I	6/2/94	8/17/94	6/30/99
Urban Development (1)									
Third municipal development	Active	S	S	Nonrisky	Satisfactory	I	3/31/92	8/3/92	6/30/99
Water Supply and Sanitation (3)									
Water, sewerage, and sanitation	Completed	S	S	Actual	Satisfactory	I	6/28/90	1/15/91	12/31/97
Second Manila sewerage	Active	S	U	Nonrisky	Highly satisfactory	I	5/21/96	n.a.	12/31/01
Water district development	Active	n.a.	n.a.	Nonrisky	Satisfactory	I	9/9/97	n.a.	6/30/03

Note: For definition of abbreviations, see Table 3.
n.a. = Not available.

TABLE A.5: LIST OF ECONOMIC AND SECTOR WORK (ESW)

REPORT TITLE	ECONOMIC OR SECTOR REPORT	DATE	REPORT #
Agriculture (8)			
Sugarlands diversification study	SR	05/30/86	6042
Agricultural sector memorandum	SR	06/01/86	6250
Agriculture: its present condition and future needs	SR	02/01/87	6613
Agrarian reform issues: an assessment of the proposal for an accelerated land reform program	SR	05/01/87	6779
Agricultural sector strategy review	SR	10/01/87	6819
Forestry, fisheries, and agricultural resource management study (FFARM study)	SR	01/01/89	7388
Irrigated agriculture sector review	SR	04/01/92	9848
Promoting equitable rural growth	SR	05/30/97	15782
Education (3)			
Education sector study – Philippines	SR	12/01/88	7473
Vocational training for operatives and craftsmen	SR	01/24/90	8259
Education financing and social equity: a reform agenda	SR	06/11/96	15898
Electric Power and Other Energy (3)			
Energy sector study	SR	09/01/88	7269
Rural electrification sector study: an integrated program to revitalize the sector	SR	11/01/89	8016
Power sector study: structural framework for the power sector	SR	11/30/94	13313
Environment (1)			
Environmental sector study toward improved environmental policies and management	SR	12/08/93	11852
Finance (3)			
Financial sector study	SR	08/01/88	7177
Regional financial sector report: lessons of financial liberalization in Asia: a comparative study	SR	11/23/88	7512
Capital market study	ER	02/01/92	10053
Industry (2)			
Issues and policies in the industrial sector	SR	07/01/87	6706
Private sector assessment (PSA)	SR	07/12/94	11853
Mining (1)			
Mining sector review	SR	10/01/87	6898
Multisector (8)			
A framework for economic recovery	ER	11/01/86	6350
Toward sustaining the economic recovery: country economic memorandum	ER	01/30/89	7438
Country economic memorandum: issues in adjustment and competitiveness	ER	10/01/90	8933
An opening for sustained growth	ER	04/01/93	11061
Infrastructure assessment study – Philippines	SR	06/01/93	11944
Recent macroeconomic developments and reform efforts	ER	06/30/94	13109
Strengthening economic resiliency	ER	11/08/96	15985
Managing global integration	SR	11/17/97	17024
Population, Health, and Nutrition (2)			
New directions in the Philippines family planning program	SR	10/01/91	9579
Devolution and health services: managing risks and opportunities	SR	05/23/94	12343
Poverty (2)			
The challenge of poverty	ER	10/01/88	7144
A strategy to fight poverty	SR	11/13/95	14933
Public Sector Management (6)			
Key issues in the nonfinancial public corporate sector: a special economic report	ER	06/01/86	6338
Selected issues in public resource management	ER	04/01/88	6887
Country economic report: public sector resource mobilization and expenditure management	ER	02/01/92	10056
Fiscal decentralization study	SR	01/01/93	10716
Public expenditure management for sustained and equitable growth	SR	09/05/95	14680
An agenda for the reform of the social security institutions	SR	09/29/95	13400
Transportation (1)			
Transport sector review	SR	03/31/88	7098

Note: Reports include only formal ESW outputs.

TABLE A.6: BANK SENIOR MANAGEMENT RESPONSIBLE FOR PHILIPPINES SINCE 1985

FISCAL YEAR	VICE PRESIDENT	DEPARTMENT OR COUNTRY DIRECTOR	FISCAL YEAR	VICE PRESIDENT	DEPARTMENT OR COUNTRY DIRECTOR
1985	Attila Karaossmanoglu	Gautam Kaji	1992	Gautam Kaji	Callisto Madavo
1986	Attila Karaossmanoglu	Gautam Kaji	1993	Gautam Kaji	Callisto Madavo
1987	Attila Karaossmanoglu	Gautam Kaji	1994	Gautam Kaji	Callisto Madavo
1988	Attila Karaossmanoglu	Gautam Kaji	1995	Russell Cheetham	Callisto Madavo
1989	Attila Karaossmanoglu	Gautam Kaji	1996	Russell Cheetham	Callisto Madavo[1]
1990	Attila Karaossmanoglu	Gautam Kaji	1997	Russell Cheetham	Javad Khalilzadeh-Shirazi
1991	Attila Karaossmanoglu	Gautam Kaji	1998	Jean-Michel Severino	Vinay K. Bhargava

Note: There was a change in the organizational structure of the Bank in FY88 when the vice presidencies for East Asia and South Asia were merged. In FY93 this arrangement ended when the two regions were again split into separate vice presidencies.
1. Division Chiefs act as Director in last three months of the year.

ANNEX B: THE PHILIPPINES: FROM CRISIS TO OPPORTUNITY/MANAGEMENT RESPONSE

Major OED Recommendations	*Management Response*
Strengthening Economic Management ESW, policy advice, technical assistance, and resumed adjustment lending are recommended for: (i) emergency assistance to help ease the current liquidity crunch; (ii) strengthening the banking sector (legal, regulatory, and supervisory regimes and failure resolution), and the capital markets (management of short-term capital flows, housing finance, and pension reform); (iii) restructuring expenditures in favor of higher public investment and maintenance expenditures, implementing civil service reform, and improving local government finance; and (iv) further reduction in import tariffs. For sectors with appropriate policy and institutional frameworks, the seal of approval of regular Public Expenditure Reviews (PERs) should open the door to sectoral investment loans and adaptable program loans with low conditionalities. A study and subsequent support for judicial system reform are also recommended.	This is largely consistent with the CAS Progress Report submitted to the Board on 3/3/98 for discussion on 3/24/98, which proposes (i) adjustment lending as well as lines of credit that would, among other things, address liquidity constraints; (ii) more emphasis on the banking sector through adjustment and TA operations, covering both the banking and nonbanking financial sector, as well as a PHRD grant for financial sector training and TA; and (iii) public sector reform and expenditure management in the context of upcoming adjustment lending, in addition to intensive work on local government finance in ongoing projects and others under preparation. The policy dialogue with the government has included discussions on a tariff reduction strategy. Instead of regular PERs, we are pursuing sectoral program reviews in view of their greater cost-effectiveness and receptivity by the client. Adaptable program loans are already under preparation in the urban, rural, and transport sectors. The government has so far not approached the Bank for support for judicial system reform, but we would respond positively to any request from the new administration.

Expanding Private Sector and Infrastructure Development
The Bank could resume *financial intermediary loans.* Learning from others' experience, the Bank could resume microcredit with simple financial products, supported by market-oriented technical assistance.

Intensified technical assistance is needed to complete regulatory reform for private participation in all infrastructure sectors. Bank Group support—including conditional sectoral lending—is necessary to achieve privatization quickly in NPC, water supply and sanitation, and transport.

The Bank could scale-up its successful lending for *Municipal Development*, including capacity building.

This is a useful suggestion in the current circumstances. As the CAS Progress Report indicates, we are looking into the possibility for new financial intermediary operations; a preparation mission is currently in the field.

We agree that continued technical assistance for further regulatory reforms and privatization is needed. This is part of our sectoral policy dialogue, investment projects, and the subject of planned sector work on government-owned corporations. We are coordinating closely with ADB to avoid overlap.

Agreed and already in line with our current assistance strategy, which focuses on lending to and capacity building of local government units (LGUs), including municipal governments, with increasing emphasis on poorer and smaller LGUs. Specific operations are under preparation.

Accelerating Rural Development and Poverty Reduction
An agreed new sector development and assistance strategy targeting the rural poor is required along the lines of recent Bank ESW for rural development.

The Bank could expand its support for land reform beyond assistance to the beneficiaries by including direct budgetary support for the completion of the final phase of land reform.

With adjustment and sector lending, the Bank could support tariff reductions for cereals, remove the rice monopoly, promote rice exports, and foster private participation in production, marketing, and distribution.

Agreed. The rural development strategy was completed in 1997 and widely discussed with all stakeholders. This is the basis for the Bank's current preparation of a Sector Assistance Strategy Note, which will include plans for an expansion of activities in the rural development sector.

Our current approach focuses on assistance to beneficiaries through ongoing projects. Direct budgetary support would likely be in support of the high costs of land acquisition (estimated at over US$1 billion) and cannot be financed by the Bank [OP 12.00, para. 2(b)].

Currently not requested or foreseen. These issues are currently largely subject of discussions with the World Trade Organization (WTO) and ADB in the context of an ADB sector reform loan. In the interest of focus and selectivity of the Bank's strategy and effective donor coordination, we are addressing these issues through our ongoing policy dialogue.

Revisiting Human Development
The continued availability of softer money from other donors and their interest in lending to social sectors could justify the Bank's stepping aside as lender, while keeping its important analytical and advisory role.

Should the Bank remain an active lender in the sector, family planning and primary health are priorities. In education, the Bank should limit its involvement with vocational and tertiary education to an advisory role.

This would be premature. The Bank has been one of the largest funding agencies in the education sector and there is continued interest in Bank lending. In the health sector, our more limited lending is demand driven, with cofinancing to achieve more concessional terms.

The Bank can be more effective (i) in the health sector by providing support not only to FP and primary care, but to reorienting delivery and financing of all public health services in the decentralized government structure and building capacity at the local level and (ii) in education, by maintaining the primary education focus, but exploring support in other subsectors to promote reforms regarding subsidies and private sector involvement.

Mobilizing Partnerships
Enhance participation of NGOs and civil society in the Bank's strategy; its wide dissemination is recommended.

Successful aid coordination by the Bank could be taken to a higher plane to maximize long-term sources of foreign savings and to achieve better results on the ground at the sectoral level. A truly participatory CAS covering all major donors should be the Bank's goal by 1999.

Agreed. We are planning to discuss Country and Sectoral Assistance Strategy Notes, prepared to build up to the FY99 CAS, with stakeholders in each sector. The resident mission has a strong outreach program to promote participation in all aspects of our work, including dialogue, ESW, and lending.

A participatory CAS is already planned, involving stakeholders. The preparation will also take full account of other donors' activities. A joint donor CAS will, however, not be possible under current conditions: such an effort would first require government leadership, high-level commitment in other donor agencies, and additional resources for the Philippines program.

ANNEX C: REPORT FROM CODE/COMMITTEE ON DEVELOPMENT EFFECTIVENESS

The Philippines: Country Assistance Review (CAR)

On March 11, 1998, the Committee on Development Effectiveness (CODE) reviewed a report prepared by the Operations Evaluation Department (OED) entitled *The Philippines: Country Assistance Review* (CAR) (SecM98-165), together with a draft management response prepared by the Philippines Headquarters Unit (EACPQ). The Committee welcomed the opportunity to discuss the CAR in advance of the Board review of the Philippines CAS Progress Report and commended OED for the effort to produce a very good and useful document in a timely manner. In particular, the Committee commended OED for ensuring that the observations about the Philippines were made in a regional context. The Committee noted that, due to the severe time constraint, OED has not been able to obtain the country's official comments on the CAR. It looks forward to the CAR's being finalized after further discussions with the Government and the Region.

The Committee appreciated the historical perspective provided in the CAR and welcomed the finding that during the past 12 years, Bank assistance has been both relevant and satisfactory at the macro level, and in some areas of private sector (including SME) development, financial sector strengthening, and municipal development, but noted with concern that its relevance and efficacy have been uneven in other sectors such as water and sanitation, transport, health, education, agriculture, and energy. The Committee also noted that the assistance strategy has moved effectively from economic recovery to poverty alleviation in line with government and Bank priorities, but that the shift is not yet complete. The CAR recommends that to help the economy reach its growth potential, fortify its resilience to domestic and global exigencies, and reduce poverty faster, the government must pursue and deepen its unfinished reform agenda.

The challenge for the government is fivefold: strengthen economic management; expand private sector and infrastructure development; accelerate rural development and attack poverty aggressively; revisit human development; and mobilize partnerships. The CAR recommends that supporting the government in pursuing this medium-term agenda should be the central tenet of the Bank's assistance strategy. The Committee welcomed management's assertion that several of the recommendations in the CAR have been incorporated into the program of lending and nonlending activities for the Philippines, as reflected in the CAS Progress Report. Others will feed into the sector strategy notes that are being prepared as background for the full CAS scheduled for next year. Several specific issues relevant to the Board discussion of the CAS Progress Report were raised during the Committee's discussion and are highlighted below.

Bank Group Role in Specific Sectors

The Committee asked for clarification of OED's finding that the continued availability of softer money from other donors and their interest in lending to social sectors could justify the Bank's stepping aside as lender in these sectors. In OED's view, since the government prefers not to borrow from the Bank for soft sectors, the Bank should respond by focusing lending on other sectors such as infrastructure, while continuing to provide analytical and advisory services in the social sectors. OED also offered the opinion that the Bank's overall performance would have been better had it concentrated lending in fewer sectors. The Committee noted management's response that to retreat from the social sectors would be premature. The Bank has been one of the largest funding agencies in the education sector, and there is continued interest in Bank lending in this area. In the health sector, the Bank's more limited lending is demand driven, usually with cofinancing to achieve more concessional terms.

The Committee was interested in the Bank's activities in and lessons learned from experience in the financial sector. OED reported that the overall impact of the Bank's assistance to the financial sector has been satisfactory. But the financial deepening and strengthening in the Philippines has some way to go. The sector still suffers from weaknesses in the regulatory and supervisory regime. Therefore, OED recommends that ESW, policy advice, technical assistance, and adjustment lending be used to strengthen further the banking sector. The Committee was satisfied that the CAS Progress Report proposes more emphasis on the banking sector through adjustment and technical assistance (TA) operations, covering both the banking and nonbanking financial sector, as well as a PHRD grant for financial sector training and TA.

Dissemination of ESW

The Committee was concerned about the finding that even though the Bank's diagnosis of the Philippines' ills has been correct, based on solid ESW, the problems with dissemination and time have limited the effectiveness and impact of ESW. Key middle and senior managers in government, parliamentary committee chairmen, business leaders, former cabinet members, and prominent intellectuals are frequently unaware of the content and, sometimes, of the existence of nonsensitive Bank reports. The Committee took note of the response that with the decentralization of management to the Philippines, a greater effort is being made to disseminate ESW information, including the establishment of a public information center.

Partnerships, Aid Coordination, and a Joint CAS

In order to deepen reform and achieve sustainable poverty reduction, OED suggests that a new compact among the government, the NGOs, the Bank, and the rest of the donor community is needed to mobilize and use external assistance effectively. The Committee welcomed the finding that the Bank has played a key role in coordinating and building consensus among donors and the government through regular dialogues. But even more important, the Bank supported the government's efforts to improve its own capacity and to assume an increasingly assertive role in aid coordination. However, even with a high level of aid coordination in evidence, OED found that there is much friendly but ultimately wasteful competition, especially in lending to the social sectors, and little reciprocal concern about other donors' results. The Committee was not supportive of the recommendation that the Bank should aim for a joint CAS covering all major donors by 1999. The view was expressed that it would not be appropriate for the Board

to review and pass judgment on a document that explicitly includes the assistance strategies of donors. Instead, the Committee agreed with management that a participatory CAS involving stakeholders should be prepared, and that the preparation should take full account of donors' activities.

The Committee raised the issue of the Bank's comparative advantage vis-a-vis the Asian Development Bank (ADB), and wanted to know how decisions were made about where the Bank focuses its activities. It noted the response that the decentralization of management to the resident mission has contributed significantly to better coordination between the ADB and the Bank. To avoid overlap, consultation at the Regional Vice President and project levels was now the norm.

Negative Net Transfers

The Committee noted the high level of total net resource flows out of the Philippines to the Bank (US$2.7 billion from 1986 to 1997). It also noted OED's view that a large negative resource flow at this still early stage of the Philippines' development raises the question of the wisdom of phasing out adjustment lending in the mid–1990s, with an agenda of structural reform still incomplete. OED further pointed out that public infrastructure investment is a severe constraint to growth. The opinion was expressed by the Committee that the question of whether adjustment lending should be resumed or not should be based on the reform effort and commitment of the government, and not on a desire to reverse the net outflow of capital from the Philippines to the Bank.

Leonard Good
Vice Chairman
CODE

OPERATIONS EVALUATION DEPARTMENT PUBLICATIONS

The Operations Evaluation Department (OED), an independent evaluation unit reporting to the World Bank's executive directors, rates the development impact and performance of all the Bank's completed lending operations. Results and recommendations are reported to the executive directors and fed back into the design and implementation of new policies and projects. In addition to the individual operations and country assistance programs, OED evaluates the Bank's policies and processes.

Operations evaluation studies, World Bank discussion papers, and all other documents are available from the World Bank InfoShop.

Summaries of studies and the full text of the *Précis* and *Lessons & Practices* can be read on the Internet at http://www.worldbank.org/html/oed/index.htm

How to Order OED Publications

Documents listed with a stock number and price code may be obtained through the World Bank's mail order service or from its InfoShop in downtown Washington, DC. For information on all other documents, contact the World Bank InfoShop.

Ordering World Bank Publications

Customers in the United States and in territories not served by any of the Bank's publication distributors may send publication orders to:

The World Bank
P.O. Box 960
Herndon, VA 20172-0960
Fax: (703) 661-1501
Telephone: (703) 661-1580
The address for the World Bank publication database on the Internet is: http://www.worldbank.org
From the World Bank homepage, select *publications*.
E-mail: pic@worldbank.org
Fax number: (202) 522-1500
Telephone number: (202) 458-5454

The World Bank InfoShop serves walk-in customers only. The InfoShop is located at:

701 18th Street, NW
Washington, DC 20433, USA

All other customers must place their orders through their local distributors.

Ordering via E-Mail

If you have an established account with the World Bank, you may transmit your order via electronic mail on the Internet to: books@worldbank.org. Please include your account number, billing and shipping addresses, the title and order number, quantity, and unit price for each item.